FIFTY YEARS IN EVERY STREET

THE ROUND HOUSE, EVERY STREET

From a drawing by L. S. Lowry
reproduced with his kind permission

FIFTY YEARS
IN EVERY STREET

THE STORY OF THE
MANCHESTER UNIVERSITY
SETTLEMENT

by

MARY D. STOCKS

SECOND EDITION
WITH AN ADDITIONAL CHAPTER ON THE
YEARS 1945–1955, BY

BRIAN RODGERS

MANCHESTER UNIVERSITY PRESS

Published by the University of Manchester at
THE UNIVERSITY PRESS
316–324, Oxford Road, Manchester, 13

First Edition . 1945
Second Edition . 1956

Printed in Great Britain by Butler & Tanner Ltd., Frome and London

FOREWORDS

NO. I

THE normal purpose of a foreword is, I suppose, to explain or commend the story that follows. Accordingly, most people wisely leave it unread, for if the story is a good one it will explain itself, if the author is well known her name will be sufficient commendation, and if obscure presumably it is the name of the writer of the foreword rather than anything he says in it that is expected to make the book go.

This foreword, having clearly an abnormal purpose, is written in the hope that most people will forsake their usual practice and read it, for it aims at saying something the author has not said and, greatly daring, at saying it better than even she could have said it, had she tried.

Fifty Years in Every Street pays tribute in turn to a number of men and women that have left a name behind them. In the chapters covering the years 1924–36, which include the second golden age of the Settlement's history, there appears pre-eminently and justly the name of J. L. Stocks. And yet that suggests but a half-truth, for J. L. Stocks's contribution to Ancoats was not just the contribution of a gifted and enthusiastic individual, it was that far more effective thing, the contribution of one member of a happy equal partnership. Mrs. Stocks's own gifts were always at the direct disposal of the Settlement, a debt to which, in my view, an occasional footnote in the text referring to plays specially written for the Round House stage pays inadequate tribute. But apart altogether from this, no one who knows the demands that a Settlement naturally makes on a Chairman's time and the inroads on his home life can doubt that what each member of the Stocks partnership gave to Ancoats was immeasurably richer for their joint contribution of time, thought and energy.

The story commends itself, and will be read with delight not only by those who know the Settlement in Ancoats but by interested workers in other fields.

G. A. SUTHERLAND.

December, 1944.

NO. II

NEARLY fifty years ago I made my contact with the Manchester Settlement through its Debating Society. I was beginning to wish to speak in public and thought that among working men in Ancoats inexperience would be treated leniently and failure forgiven. So I adventured. I remember my first debate. Two only of the speakers had volubility and they were both Scotsmen with whom later I made friends. One of them was a natural speaker whose gift was reinforced by wide reading. He knew the Bible and John Stuart Mill and Macaulay and expounded Radical individualism with force and the dignity that belonged to his studious type. The other was a bearded Highlander who spoke fiercely about something or other. But he was handicapped by an accent unintelligible to Southern ears and an excruciating vocal pitch. His grievance [often ventilated at later meetings and jocularly said to be against " ta clan Mactavish "] was never understood. The audience respected his sincerity and warmly applauded him—when he sat down. I fell in love with the Debating Society and met there famous men : G. K. C. for instance. Chesterton proposed " The Abolition of the Inevitable " and afterwards commented audibly on the utterances of those who differed from him. Someone said : " Mr. Chesterton's arguments won't hold water."—" Mr. Chesterton will," retorted G. K. C. and took an appropriate swig. He was a mountain of merriment. The Debates are a fragrant recollection, particularly as regards the interventions of the President, Harold Pilkington-Turner, who really sustained them. Members of the Society thought and said that Turner's place was Westminster, and indeed his oratory was nobly phrased and always touched with a humour at which even passion and rancour would relax.

After a space my interest passed from the Debates to the wider world of the rapidly developing Settlement. The pioneer Wardens, Helen Stoehr and E. T. Campagnac, had been succeeded by Alice Crompton under whose impact the Settlement became aglow. Alice Crompton was an exceptional leader. She swept into Ancoats like a wind. Someone said that she brought hope like a relief column and reassurance like a grant-in-aid. She vibrated with energy and purpose and was loved for her sympathy and grace. She upreared a banner and called a crusade. And crusaders responded. From the University and the *Manchester Guardian* especially, gifted men were drawn to Ancoats: among others, Tout, Weiss, Chapman, Hartog, Powicke, Hobhouse, Ensor, and Laurence Scott whose early death was a universal bereavement. T. C. Horsfall, a civic saint who founded the Art Museum, and taught us to loathe jerry builders, was already attached; so was Pilkington-Turner. Sydney MacDougall, Guy Kendall and T. R. Marr were a succession of co-Wardens. Round these stalwarts stood the rest of us; and, notably, gifted women: Helen Fisher, Ellen Creak, Beatrice Vernon, and later on Emily Jenkinson and Janet Blair. Teresa Billington, who won renown as an eloquent Suffragette leader, and I, ran the Settlement Associates, one hundred and fifty of them, who were the " storm troops " of the Settlement. A score of these admirable associates deserve to be named, but Albert Robinson, a really expert organizer, Paddy Ryan, full of Irish good-humour and most un-Irish technical accomplishments, Fred Helliwell, who only conversed when he was not allowed to sing Schumann or Schubert or recite Matthew Arnold, were the outstanding ones. Perhaps I should also include Bruno Lasker, a German—half poet and half economist—who on a wise premonition had fled his native land. Bruno's delight, when he had money, which was seldom, was to give flowers to the poor neighbours of the Settlement and he would expound lovely, original, and entirely impracticable ideas. This impressive and dedicated, if somewhat motley, host followed the Wardens with ecstasy —they were sons of God shouting for joy. In divers ways they aided an achievement which with some knowledge of the work of institutions in Britain and U.S.A. I think to have been extraordinary. It was a many-sided achievement. It began with a People's University: Kendall expounded Plato; and Turner, Shelley and Keats. Marr taught Civics and Hobhouse Sociology. Chapman had a devoted body of students of economics. Hartog was able to make working men write good English, and Ellen Creak read and enlarged upon Dante to a rapt following of young women. In the background was Ensor, from whom information could be obtained—on anything. Recreation followed education. Ancoats attended our At Homes on Tuesdays and our dances democratically governed on Saturdays. Beatrice Vernon's Friday entertainments drew hundreds of children. Once monthly Helen Fisher's Santa Fina Party conveyed the crippled people of the neighbourhood : in summer to some country garden, or, in winter, to the Settlement. Then there were Court and Alley Concerts. A peripatetic piano was wheeled to a slum made gay with preparatory bunting. Musicians arrived, played and sang and set the slum singing. The Settlement Dramatic Society concentrated on Shakespeare. It was so good that Ellen Terry heard of it and on a never-to-be-forgotten evening came and read Rosalind to its members, some of whom were said to have swooned with happiness. The great actress was a great lady and later in the week invited the society to see her play, and, what they valued even more, treated them as dear friends. Even Education and Recreation mattered less to us than Reform. Twice Albert Robinson's investigation staff revealed the existence of large-scale unemployment and inspired remedial action by the City Council. Roused by Horsfall and Marr we campaigned against bad housing. Under a non-party banner we went into local politics and in a conflict which seemed to us to make history carried T. R. Marr, our housing candidate, to the City Council. We formulated a municipal programme and explained it at local street corners. We demonstrated— we were always demonstrating. Turmoil ceased at the week-ends which—were welcome. They brought a breathing space and an opportunity for refreshment ; then the Field Club, 50 or 60 strong, followed Weiss or some other eminent botanist in a search for specimens ; then our sports section took the field ; then a merry party visited the Associates' cottage at Hayfield (short week-end 2s. 6d.), talked poetry or staged a Shakespearian scene in romantic surroundings, strolled about and often slept upon the moors.

More than most human institutions a Settlement goes up and down. Its circle is held together by affection which is vulnerable to the attack of time and change. As members of the circle withdraw or age " glad confident morning recedes " and resolution falters. A new call is needed to a new crusade. In this respect the Manchester Settlement is fortunate. For it has been several times revivified and several times has recaptured the faith and ardour in which it began. Hilda Cashmore was one who rekindled its fires and she and J. L. and Mary Stocks are among its canonized names. Just now in its time of Jubilee the Settlement is again undergoing re-birth and with vivid leadership is touching new areas of Manchester in each of which in due time it will blossom and fructify. The survivors of my generation, not numerous now, to whom their days in the Settlement are still a precious memory will wish Manchester to cherish and endow more richly than before an incomparable institution.

As I finish this foreword to a very vivid and charming book which increases the debt of the Settlement, already immense, to Mrs. Stocks, I hear that an old friend of the Settlement has died in America and bequeathed to it some £500—the bulk of his worldly goods.

I am touched to hear of the death of this donor, for I well remember his appearing at the Settlement, shy, lonely and inarticulate ; and the way in which the influences of the Settlement played upon and cheered him and the extent to which he loved the Settlement and regarded it as impeccable and sanctified. He would gladly undertake any service, trivial or even menial, for the Settlement. He would for example sweep a room, and although frail, essay to carry to a conveyance some member of the Santa Fina party not easily portable and as heavy as himself. How he came to leave Manchester I do not know, but I am sure that his severance from the Settlement would cut him to the heart and be a continuing regret, and that, in unaccustomed surroundings, the loneliness from which the Settlement rescued him long ago, would return and distress him ; and I am still more sure that in his new environment the thought of the Settlement would be more than ever dear to him and that he would many times call up a vision of it and remember its voices. And most of all I know that the thought that he would be able substantially to help the Settlement would be pleasing to him and a source of deep joy.

J. J. MALLON.

PREFACE TO THE SECOND EDITION

THE first edition of *Fifty Years in Every Street* was published during 1945, when the Manchester University Settlement celebrated its fiftieth birthday. Now, ten years later, and to mark the Diamond Jubilee, Dr. Mary Stocks has graciously permitted the publication of a second edition with an additional chapter by Mr. Brian Rodgers which covers the post-war years 1945–55.

We are grateful to Mr. Rodgers for demonstrating so clearly, interestingly and with such insight the altered circumstances which emerged after the fighting ceased and whilst the Welfare State was evolving and developing. The reconstitution of the work, the new problems which appeared, the changing character of the service, the influence of the purchase of a second-hand bus—which made possible visits to the continent—and the financial crises which seem inseparable from such work are all fully discussed. In fact we are brought right up to date and encouraged to peep into the future.

I commend this human story, not only to all friends of the Settlement, but to everyone who is concerned with social work ; it is an inspiring history which is most happily told.

JOHN S. B. STOPFORD.

CONTENTS

ILLUSTRATIONS

CHAPTER I

MODERN economic historians have pointed out that every social organism carries within itself the germs of its own decay. Alternatively, one might say that every social organism contains living tissues whose growth will in the end transform it, by a process of response to the changing needs of its environment, into something essentially different, though superficially recognizable by name and outward form. Our choice between the words "decay" and "growth" will be to some extent conditioned by our attitude to change and our attachment to familiar ways. And, of course, by our angle of approach. Green mould, which is a reproach to last year's jam, may be a crown of glory to the cheese, or alternatively the starting point of fruitful experiment in the bio-chemist's laboratory.

Examples of this process in the sphere of social service are not far to seek. Miss Octavia Hill's highly individualized system of house-property management, for example, contained within itself a germ of municipal socialism which was no part of her vision of a happier world. To the end of her life she cherished a profound mistrust of State action and would probably have looked dubiously upon the spread of direct State provision of subsidized homes which has occurred since her death. Yet she forged a magnificent instrument for the ordered progress of such enterprise by her technique of management, and provided an unanswerable argument for its expansion by her spectacular demonstration that slum-dwellers are made by slums rather than slums by slum-dwellers. Thus the self-dedicated Victorian philanthropists who collected Miss Octavia's rents are the ancestors of an expanding army of trained and certificated officers of statutory authorities. What is left of her system ? There would be much truth in the reply : " The living tissue of it."

In no sphere of voluntary activity has this interlocked

process of decay and growth been more active than in the philanthropic development which we may call the Settlement movement, since it sprang from a paper entitled *Settlements of University Men in Great Towns*, read in St. John's College, Cambridge, by an East End parson called Samuel Barnett. That momentous reading occurred in 1883, and from the discussions which followed it there emerged an activity : the founding of Toynbee Hall in Whitechapel, which was destined to give a new direction to Victorian philanthropy, and open up a more accurate conception among the well-to-do classes of the stresses and strains of working-class life. The settlers who followed Barnett to Whitechapel could not share the weekly-wage anxiety of their neighbours, nor were they required to experience at first hand the horrors of dirt and overcrowding, untended sickness and uncultivated minds. But as near neighbours, breathing the same smutty air, seeing the same unappetizing sights, and using at full stretch the imagination which had brought them there, they were able vicariously to suffer these things, and to gain from their vicarious suffering both new impetus towards the ends of social reform and new skill in devising precise means to those ends. And therein lay the germ of the Settlement movement : of its decay or its growth according to one's angle of vision.

From activities born of an intense pre-occupation with the quality of individual personal relationships, there emerged through half a century, a growing consciousness of the limitations of individual reforming zeal. Year by year the Settlements played their zealous part in the building up of our statutory social services. The personal experiences of the settlers helped to mould their shape and speed their growth. It was from researches conducted as a Toynbee Hall settler that William Beveridge hammered out his thesis that unemployment is primarily a problem of industry rather than a problem of personal character or particular misfortune. It was from personal encounters between the sweated workers of East London and a group of Oxford settlers, that the sweated industries campaign generated the impetus which led to the tentative reappearance of statutory wage regulation in 1909, and the Manchester Settlement produced the man who carried that campaign to fruition. There is indeed scarcely any field of social legislation or any statutory instrument of social service which does not owe something of its inception or direction to the recorded observations or voluntary pioneer experiments of settlers, who year by year followed the call of Samuel Barnett to those mean streets where their fellow-citizens led arxious, meagre lives. Must we regard this process as one of growth or decay?

It has, of course, transformed both the activities and personnel of the settlements into something new and strange. Much of what they once did for their neighbours is now done—and more comprehensively if not better done— by statutory bodies. There are fewer voluntary spare-time philanthropists among the settlers. Their place is taken by salaried officers of the State, the local authorities, or the non-statutory social service organizations. There is scarcely a settlement activity which is not at some point interlocked with a statutory service, for which the settlement may act as agent with appropriate financial backing. Even such voluntary spare-time settlers as remain are largely concerned with the performance of statutory functions, serving as magistrates, care committee workers, and members of Trade Boards. And the settlements themselves are functioning to an ever-increasing extent as recognized training agencies for not abnormally altruistic men and women, who seek careers in social service and are engaged in acquiring the necessary diplomas and certificates.

Here, then, are clear and abundant signs of growth. What of the decay? The answer depends upon whether it is possible to realize the limitations of social reform based on the personal services of individual human beings to other individual human beings, without losing faith in the profound importance of individual personal relationships as a qualitative element in good citizenship. The early settlers were, by deliberate and declared policy, no mere dispensers of charitable relief. But their activities were none the less charitable. The word " charity " has been battered out of recognition by hack use; it has been hardened by familiar association with a scientific approach to the problem of destitution, involving the prudent segregation of the deserving from the undeserving. It has been softened by familiar application to trivial soul-saving almsgiving. But in its origins it is a beautiful and gracious word, and an alternative familiarity indicates it as a " most excellent gift ". In its application to the personal relationship of man to man—which is where it properly belongs—we may still regard it as " the very bond of peace and of all virtues ". It was this " most excellent gift " that led generations of settlers to the nether regions of our great towns in the wake of Samuel Barnett. They found there the privation and squalor and human endurance which they had nerved themselves to find. They acquired there a capacity for service sharpened by new knowledge and community of thought, which they had hoped to acquire. They enjoyed there a wealth of varied and vitalizing interest, colour, humour and cheer, which they had scarcely expected to enjoy.

It is with the story of one such social adventure in the heart of an Industrial Revolution slum that we are now concerned. Let us, therefore, in imagination, turn on the gas lights, recall Victoria to her monumental throne, revive our tarnished faith in the inevitable progress of mankind to ordered democratic decency, and tune our ears to the clatter of clogs on stone and the clank of cotton mills. We are bound for Manchester and fifty years ago. Skies are sulphurous and streets are foul there, but the spirit of social service is wide awake and what Oxford University did for Whitechapel in 1885, Owens College is determined to do for Ancoats in 1894.

CHAPTER II

ANCOATS PAST AND PRESENT

IT must not be regarded as a general rule that what London does to-day Manchester will do to-morrow; but in the matter of University Settlement activity this unusual sequence did in fact occur. The work of Barnett and his friends at Toynbee Hall was read about and talked about and inwardly digested wherever social conscience, intelligence, and imagination worked in combination. Thus at the opening of the Session 1894, the Principal of Owens College—now the University of Manchester—gave utterance to the view that members of his College were playing an insufficient part in philanthropic work at a time when "the participation in these works of communities as such lent to them an extraordinary accession of impulse". The fact, said Dr. Ward, that Owens College represented no church or sect, no faction or fraction, that it was based on the breadth and freedom of principle which inspired its founder, should augment rather than diminish the weight of its responsibility towards "the claims of the poor, the sick, the suffering, the neglected, the outcast, pressing upon one another as they did in dolorous competition".

Dr. Ward's address anticipated by a few months a meeting held at Toynbee Hall to discuss the extension to other large centres of population of University Settlements on the London model. Thus he was able to inform that meeting of what Manchester intended to do instead of waiting to be told what Manchester ought to do. It was, however, no part of Manchester's intention to act in isolation. Canon Barnett, Warden of Toynbee Hall, was invited to come North, and a meeting convened by a group of former Owens College students, was called for the purpose of hearing him, in the rooms of the College Union on March 27th, 1895, under the chairmanship of Dr. Ward. The meeting was duly held, and at its close two resolutions were passed.

5

Since they proclaim the genesis of the Manchester Settlement and indicate its spiritual paternity they deserve to be quoted in full :—

(1) That this meeting recognizes the desirability of setting on foot an organization of social work in Manchester, in the spirit of the University Settlements Scheme as explained by Canon Barnett and the Right Hon. Sir John Gorst ; such work to be, if possible, connected closely, though not exclusively, with Owens College ; and that those present are prepared to use their best endeavours in the furtherance of this object.

(2) That a General Committee consisting of those present, with power to add to their number, be formed for the purpose of taking the initial steps requisite for carrying the first resolution into effect ; and that this Committee shall at a subsequent meeting elect an Executive Committee ; and that Messrs. A. Woodroofe Fletcher and H. Pilkington Turner be requested to act as Honorary Secretaries, *pro tem.*, of the General Committee.

In due course the General Committee gave place to the elected Executive Committee, complete with officers. Its Hon. Secretaries remained the same. Dr. Ward became President ; T. C. Horsfall, J.P., Chairman, until a few months later pressure of public work caused him to give place to Professor Tout ; and George Milner, J.P., Treasurer. The Committee consisted of Professor Samuel Alexander, Dr. Annie Anderson, Miss Alice Cooke, Dr. T. A. Goodfellow, J. W. Graham, Alfred Haworth, Miss Edith Lang, J. Ernest Phythian, Miss Esther Roper, Charles Rowley, Miss Marie Southern, Miss C. H. Stoehr and Professor Tout. To those well acquainted with the academic and civic history of Manchester the names are significant, for they show the weight of support behind the Settlement project.

Throughout the summer months of 1895 organization proceeded. An offer by T. C. Horsfall of rooms in the Ancoats Art Museum was a big step forward. Miss C. H. Stoehr and Dr. Annie Anderson went into residence there on October 4th—thus giving the Settlement a local habita-

tion. In due course a group of men residents gathered at
17, Manor Street, Ardwick, and with the appointment of
Ernest T. Campagnac the Settlement acquired a Warden.
Less than a year later, at its first Annual General Meeting
on July 15th, 1896, it acquired also a Constitution. The
first clause of this Constitution confers upon the Settlement
a name by which it was not hereafter to be known. " That
the name of this Association," so runs Clause 1, " shall be
the University Settlement, Manchester." For years it has
been known as the Manchester University Settlement, and
more briefly to its friends, as the M.U.S.

But the preamble to the Constitution was of more permanent application. " This Settlement," so runs the preamble, " is founded in the hope that it may become common
ground on which men and women of various classes may
meet in goodwill, sympathy and friendship ; that the
residents may learn something of the conditions of an industrial neighbourhood, and share its interests, and endeavour
to live among their neighbours a simple and religious life."
That hope was realized. Many generations of settlers were
destined to find goodwill, sympathy and friendship in a
classless community ; to learn something of industrial conditions and use their knowledge in a larger world ; and amidst
those bleak conditions to live lives that were certainly simple,
and doubtless—though not by any doctrinal test—religious.

But before embarking upon the tale of their various activities some account must be given of the Settlement's first
habitation and of the neighbourhood which surrounded it.

At the close of the nineteenth century, closely packed
round the interlocked business centres of Manchester and
Salford, there lay an inner ring of densely populated slums.
Here and there it contained a street or terrace of spacious
Georgian houses, engulfed and befouled by the swift tide of
industrial progress which characterized the early years of
that expansive century. Friedrich Engels describes its
earlier appearance and historic origins in his menacing
indictment of English working-class conditions in 1844.[1]

[1] *Condition of the Working-Class in England in 1844*, by F. Engels,
trans. by F. K. Wischnewetzky. Allen & Unwin, 1926.

By the end of the century the main line railways had ploughed great furrows through the encircling gloom, sweeping away buildings and lopping off street ends in their inexorable push to the spacious outer world. To-day extensive demolition schemes, carried through by the Manchester and Salford Housing Committees gratuitously assisted by the *Luftwaffe*, have cleared wide open spaces in it. Light and air now play upon large tracts of caked brown earth strewn with bricks and rubble. But the air is still murky, and the sun, when it chooses to shine in these regions, gives a queer impression of shimmering warmth seen through smoked glasses. Of this inner ring the district known as Ancoats, and covering the New Cross Ward of Manchester City, forms a segment to the north-east. It is an area rich in historical association, emphatic in its rectangular personality, and obstinately loved by its inhabitants, many of whom have to be bribed, bullied, or blasted from their residences when circumstances render their departure unavoidable.

Friedrich Engels, writing in the "hungry forties", cites Ancoats as a region of back alleys and jerry-built mean streets. But among them, he says : "stand the largest Mills of Manchester lining the canals, colossal six and seven-storeyed buildings towering with their slender chimneys far above the low cottages of the workers. The population of the district consists, therefore, chiefly of mill-hands, and in the worst streets of hand-weavers." It is these great buildings with their tall chimneys, the regimented black waters of the Rochdale and Ashton canals, the harsh stone setts of the main roadways, the sharp fall of the ground to the winding River Medlock with its jutting eastern bank, which give to Ancoats its shape and personality. So that even those whose standards of health and comfort preclude a desire to live there, experience some stirring of æsthetic feeling if not of positive affection, when they recall its strongly contrasted planes and inescapable dour dignity.

But the "low cottages" of Engels's angry survey did not, during the course of the nineteenth century, improve with keeping nor achieve the dignity of age. Jerry-built at its beginning, they were dilapidated at its end. Back to back

houses, that evil heritage of Industrial Revolution private
enterprise acting in response to effective economic demand,
were tending to disappear under Corporation pressure. But
there were still plenty of them. Pail closets were the prevail-
ing type of sanitary inconvenience, and it was not uncommon
for a group of houses to share an outside water-tap. The
Railway Companies had been busy during the middle years
of the century, and their lines and goods yards covered many
acres. But the countryside had receded miles farther from
the city's centre with the spread of surrounding built-up
areas, and the crowded population of Ancoats was no longer,
as in the days of Mrs. Gaskell's *Mary Barton*, within easy
walking distance of the fields. The handloom weavers had,
of course, disappeared with the supersession of their obso-
lescent looms. Association with the textile industry was
maintained chiefly through daughters at the mill. Fathers
were for the most part labourers earning round about a
pound a week. " The inhabitants," says the contemporary
report [1] from which these facts are lifted, " are poor and
none of them are far removed from actual want." It is not
surprising, therefore, to encounter in Ancoats the statistical
phenomena usually associated with poverty, dirt and overcrowding. According to the Medical Officer of Health's
report for 1901, out of every 1,000 children born in Ancoats,
234 died in their first year. As compared with an average
death-rate for the Manchester area of 21·6 per 1,000, that
of Ancoats was 28·32.

Such was the district in which the Settlement pioneers of
1895 decided to settle. Their decision was governed partly
by the needs of the area and by its proximity to Owens
College. But Ancoats was not the only slum area thus
situated. It was, however, an area like the East End of
London, towards which philanthropic activities were already
directed. Charles Rowley's famous Ancoats Brotherhood
drew lecturers and artists of national repute to weekly
meetings in the New Islington Hall. But the final and
determining factor was the offer by Mr. T. C. Horsfall, of

[1] *Housing Conditions in Manchester and Salford*, by T. R. Marr,
1904.

rooms in the Ancoats Art Museum. Which shows that even at this early date Ancoats was not without cultural centres and a measure of paternal solicitude, the historical roots of which call for their share of preliminary attention.

In the days before the mechanization of the cotton industry and the great expansion of industrial activity which accompanied it, Manchester was an unincorporated township under the hereditary manorial jurisdiction of the Mosley family. Such it remained, beneath an increasingly complicated superstructure of improvised local administration, until its incorporation as a Borough in 1838. By that time the reigning Mosley no longer inhabited his hereditary manorial dwelling at Ancoats Hall on the western bank of the Medlock. But Ancoats Hall still stood on its ancient site, a spacious country house with grounds sloping down to the river, surrounded by commercial and industrial impedimenta which by the date of Manchester's incorporation had begrimed its walls, killed its surrounding vegetation, and so depressed its neighbourhood as to render it less eligible for aristocratic residence. It remained, however, a lordly two-storeyed country house with large rooms, long passages and some encircling breathing space, and at a time when mill-owners lived near their work and breathed the same air as their workpeople, it was inhabited by a well-to-do family called Murray.

Meanwhile an alternative and strangely contrasted squirearchy had established itself a few hundred yards away, on the east side of Every Street, which runs north from the main thoroughfare of Great Ancoats Street and parallel with the River Medlock. A certain James Scholefield, a herbalist of some local repute and an ardent Swedenborgian, known to his generation alternatively as Doctor Scholefield and the Rev. James Scholefield, had acquired several acres of land between Every Street and the Medlock, on which he had erected a curiously shaped building. It consisted of a small, square, two-storeyed red brick house of pleasant proportions fronting on the street. Adhering to its rear wall and connected with the house by an inside door, was a spacious circular building surmounted by a lantern, bearing over its outer entrance the title : *Christ Church*, and the date of its

completion : 1821. In this pleasing and unusual place of
worship Doctor Scholefield ministered to the souls of his
neighbours. In a surgery adjoining the church he ministered
to their bodies. In a basement schoolroom underneath it,
assisted by the surviving adult members of his family, he
ministered to their minds. In the surrounding acreage he
buried those whom he could not cure, and it may be pre-
sumed that with the revenues of this proprietary graveyard
he financed his family and his varied philanthropic activities.
Under the stimulus of a cholera epidemic, and Ancoats being
what it was, the graveyard became increasingly populous
until the Corporation, with sanitary prudence, closed it in
1855, to the great sorrow of its owner who died in that same
year. The larger part of it was subsequently developed by
his heirs as a building site for cottage property of the usual
Ancoats type. But the portion immediately surrounding the
house and chapel remained as an open space for later
generations, and it contained three features of interest, two
of which remain. The first is the tomb of the Scholefield
family, to the right of the front door directly under the
window of the doctor's parlour. With dates ranging from
1834 to 1855, its stone tablet records a devastating infant
mortality in his own family. The second, behind the
church, is a communal tombstone recording the names of
certain committee men responsible for the erection of a
monument to Orator Hunt of " Peterloo " fame. The third
is, or was—for all traces of it have since disappeared—the
Hunt monument itself, of which the foundation stone was
laid by the Chartist leader Fergus O'Connor in the spring
of 1842. It seems to have been an obelisk of some considerable size, for at a later date it was demolished by order of the
doctor's grandson-in-law, according to one report because it
had become a dangerous structure, according to another,
because it was composed of saleable material. But its
presence in the doctor's yard is an indication of his political
colour.

He was, in fact, a " left wing " man, a friend of parlia-
mentary reform and of all working class causes. Tradition
says that from an upper window of his house Cobden

addressed an Ancoats crowd. From contemporary press
records can be compiled a vivid chronicle of his contacts
with the Chartist movement during the great " turn out "
and the accompanying disorders of the early forties.[1]   The
Chartist convention of 1842 was held in his round chapel.
Its irresponsible spell-binding convener, Fergus O'Connor,
stayed in his house.   For his alleged part in these con-
spiratorial doings Scholefield was included in the Chartist
" round up " of that year and tried with the Chartist leaders
at the Lancaster Assizes in the Spring of 1843.   But there
was no case against him as an instigator to violence and he
returned to Ancoats a free man without a stain on his
character, back to his many-sided ministry and his lifelong
fight against disease and disorder, ignorance and squalor.
In fact, he was no believer in violence, nor was he primarily
a political leader.   He was a philanthropist : a pioneer
settler in a wilder, darker age.   And when a later generation
of settlers came in due course to occupy his premises, they
found there and in the surrounding streets, an elusive but
inescapable flavour of the Scholefield tradition.   His personality came readily to life among them.   With a little stretch
of imagination one could hear on dark nights, the ghostly
stampede of a Chartist crowd up Every Street—and feel,
pressing round the open space where Orator Hunt's great
obelisk once stood, the irrepressible surge of democratic faith
beating its way through the frustrating penury of the
" hungry forties ".

It was not, however, in these premises that the Manchester
University settlers made their first settlement, but in the
former home of the Mosleys and the Murrays at Ancoats
Hall, at the invitation of Mr. T. C. Horsfall whose Art
Museum was already installed there.   If their rooms are
haunted—and it has been confidently asserted that an
eighteenth-century lady walks the upper floor—it is by the
resentful spirits of the dispossessed aristocracy rather than
by the clamorous ghosts of toilers on the march.   The

[1] This incident is the subject of a play : *Dr. Scholefield*, by
M. D. Stocks (St. Ann's Press, Manchester), acted by members
of the M.U.S. in the round chapel in 1934.

atmosphere of Ancoats Hall at the time of this first settlement in it, was impregnated, however, with the spirit of John Ruskin, under whose inspiration T. C. Horsfall had begun a collection of pictures for the use of school children, in 1877. In 1886 the Manchester Art Museum Committee, which had become under Horsfall's leadership an active body for the encouragement of public interest in art and nature, secured a lease of Ancoats Hall from the Midland Railway, and installed the collection in it. What Miss Miranda Hill and the Kyrle Society were doing in London, the ardent volunteers of the Art Museum were doing in Manchester ; all that and more. The daring blues and greens, the sweeping unashamed curves of Morris's designs inspired them. The drabness of the slums challenged them. Into the Board Schools they went, painting, potting, expounding, displaying —and to them and their ever growing collection of beautiful objects in the heart of Ancoats, came flocking the children of the ugly streets. It was into this already active hive of culture that Miss Stoehr and Dr. Annie Anderson stepped on October 4th, 1895—under the Railway Bridge, up the hill, over the cobbles, round the curve of a treeless drive, and into the temple of arts and crafts. Their arrival marks the settlement of the Settlement.

CHAPTER III

THE SETTLERS AT HOME

IN the year 1885—the year in which Canon and Mrs. Barnett settled into their residence at Toynbee Hall, Miss Octavia Hill expressed grave doubts concerning the ability of the comparatively rich to live amongst the deplorably poor. " I believe myself," she wrote in a letter to her mother, " that the strain of living *in* the worst places would be too trying *yet* to educated people ; it would diminish their strength and so their usefulness. The reform must be, I believe, more gradual. . . . I should urge the spending of *many* hours weekly there, as achieving *most* just now, because it is less suicidal than the other course and more natural." Subsequent events allayed her fears. The suicide rate among settlers in slum areas proved to be negligible, while the pace of their work demonstrated the evitability of gradualness.

But if the suicide rate was negligible among settlers in Ancoats, it was not for want of petty discouragement during the first few years of the Settlement's existence. For one particular reason or another there was a rapid turnover of personnel. Finances were precarious, and the Settlement had a little housing problem of its own. Let us deal separately with these interlocked impedimenta :—

On October 4th, 1895, Miss Stoehr and Miss Anderson walked into Ancoats Hall as residents. They very soon walked out again. For reasons not recorded in contemporary reports the premises were found to be " unsuitable for the purpose " of residence. But though the first two settlers found it an unsuitable home, it continued to function as an operational headquarters for Settlement activities. Meanwhile, the men settlers had experienced no better luck. A house in Ancoats Grove, selected as their first home, was on occupation " discovered to be insanitary ". This is scarcely surprising, for Ancoats Grove was not at the time a very sanitary street. So they moved to 17 Manor Street, on the Ardwick side of Ancoats, and it was there that the first Warden came into residence. By which time the women had completed their migration and were installed at 128 Higher Ardwick—a house of grimed but gracious presence, dating from an age when Mrs. Gaskell's *Mary Barton* could still find wealth and elegance in the purlieus of Ardwick Green. So for the moment both groups were duly accommodated—but not for long, and this time, owing to financial stringency.

The first Annual Report of the Settlement, dated 1897, records a subscription list of £220 15s. 6d. and donations to the tune of £249 4s. The subscription list is significant. There were, as ever since there always have been, a few large subscribers : in this case, two twenty-pounders and five ten-pounders. In later years their names, and other names recur in subscription and donation lists, especially at moments of economic crisis. They are names familiar in the business and civic life of Manchester : Haworth, Worthington, Philips, Rylands, Horsfall, Ashton, Barlow, Lees. But for the most part, the subscription list in this first report, as in subsequent reports, is largely composed of relatively small subscriptions by persons, many of whose names appear also among those of the Settlement's active workers. At the head of the list stands the name of one of the greatest philosophers of our time : Professor Samuel Alexander. Its position is, of course, conditioned by its high alphabetical priority. But were any attempt made to regroup the list with respect to goodness, wisdom, or world-wide fame, there is little doubt that the name of Samuel Alexander could remain *in situ*.

All the same, from the practical point of view, and taking subscriptions and donations together, here was not a very adequate financial backing for so bold a venture—and with a full-time salaried warden to provide for. It is not surprising that the year's working shows a reduction of the balance in hand from £69 19s. 7d. to £21 6s. The second annual report shows a slight but insubstantial increase both of subscriptions and donations, but the balance in hand was reduced to 4d. Fourpence on the right side, indeed, but only by virtue of a serious contraction of the initial plan. After the discussion of an alternative arrangement, the women were recalled to Ancoats Hall, where they seem to have proved capable of standing up to conditions formerly deemed " unsuitable ", and the house in Higher Ardwick was given up. The second annual report for 1898–9 shows subscriptions up a little—donations heavily down. In 1899–1900, subscriptions were very slightly down, donations very slightly up. In 1900–1 subscriptions rose to £339 6s.; but donations slumped to £46, leaving an adverse balance of 7d., due to the treasurer. From 4d. in hand to 7d. in debt on a fairly static balance sheet is a discouraging four years' financial pilgrimage for any treasurer, however secure he may feel regarding the ultimate repayment of his sevenpence.

But this small figure on the debit side is not the whole financial tale of this momentous year. The turn of the century proved to be the turn of the Settlement's economic fortunes, in the shape of three gigantic special donations. The first two, £1,000 each from Mrs. Rylands and Mrs. James Worthington, enabled the Settlement to acquire the former domain of Dr. Scholefield : his house at No. 20 Every Street, and its surrounding open space, furnished not, alas, with the Hunt Memorial, but with an object of more practical import in the form of an enormous wooden structure known as the Recreation Room. With this property went the mortal remains of its earlier incumbent, together with those of his family and many of the neighbours to whom he ministered so faithfully in life and death. Their presence under the black sods of the Settlement's new estate was destined in later years to prove both a boon and an embarrassment. A boon because a recognition of their rights in death guaranteed the preservation of an open space : an embarrassment, because of certain limitations and formalities connected with the removal of their tombstones. But that belongs to a later period of reconstruction. Meanwhile, 20 Every Street became in this year of grace at the opening of our twentieth century, the home of the men residents ; the dishevelled structure of the attached " round chapel " became a source of mildly remunerative letting; and what was more important, its surrounding precincts became the Settlement's own proprietary playground. The third special donation—£500 from Miss Marjory Lees—provided Ancoats Hall with a " large bathroom and lavatory ", whose absence had doubtless been a factor in earlier complaints concerning the unsuitability of these premises for the purpose of residence. It also provided for the " complete redecoration of Ancoats Hall " and left a " considerable balance in hand " for pressing needs.

One more record of development remains to complete this inspiriting phase of settlement expansion. For six years the Settlement and the Art Museum had " kept company ". For six years they had striven for the same ideals, occupied the same premises, engaged the energies of the same workers, provided members for one another's committees, breathed the same smoky air, appealed to the same obtuse public. In November 1901 their marriage was solemnized by an agreement involving complete amalgamation under a single Constitution adopted by a combined meeting of their respective members and subscribers. The Annual Report for 1902 thus bears—as subsequent reports were destined to bear for sixteen fruitful years—the title : Manchester Art Museum and University Settlement.

Now it is obvious that developments of this kind, backed by sums so considerable, contributed by ladies of proved experience and discrimination in philanthropic affairs, do not occur in a vacuum. Behind those disappointingly static balance sheets energy must have been generating and results accumulating ; and, turning from the financial pages of the Settlement's reports to its records of work done and response evoked, it becomes clear that such was indeed the case. Nor should we be far wrong in attributing a particular significance to the emergence in those records of one name, that of Alice Crompton.

Reference has been made to the rapid turnover of personnel as one of three impedimenta to the Settlement's early progress. For nearly three years the pioneer Miss Stoehr sustained the headship of the Women's House, giving place in 1898 to Miss Alice Crompton who, with a meagre salary, accepted the title of its Warden. It was on the men's side that the turnover occurred. The first Warden of the Settlement, Mr. Campagnac, resigned with Miss Stoehr in 1898, and a successor was hard to find. In the following year the Settlement was able to share with Ruskin Hall, a short-lived attempt at a residential working men's college established at 20 Every Street, the services of Mr. Sidney McDougall. His appointment was for six months, and when it expired the Settlement was " not then in a position to appoint a permanent and independent Warden ", though Mr. McDougall continued to give unpaid help. But in 1901 it was in a position to appoint Mr. Guy Kendall for one year. It is not until the first report of the newly wedded Manchester Art Museum and University Settlement in 1902 that the name of T. R. Marr appears as Warden of the Men's House at 20 Every Street, and his coming adds an element of stability and promise to the developments of that wonderful year. But even so, much work had already been done.

It is sometimes believed that voluntary philanthropic enterprise has tended to move from a Victorian preoccupation with the relief of individual destitution to a growing concern with the higher education of politically adult persons whose primary physical needs are the proper concern of the statutory social services. The Manchester University Settlement, however, starting with the conviction that humanity has a great inheritance of ancient and world-wide culture, and that this should be shared by all, moved rather in the opposite direction. As missionaries of the magic of art, the significance of history, the wonders of science and the beauty of nature, its workers found themselves increasingly preoccupied with attempts to straighten out the bodies of those whose minds they were cultivating, and reorder an economic environment which was clearly inimical to the increase of spiritual and mental perception. Without the co-operation or stimulus of the Workers' Educational Association, which did not at this time exist, it was, at the outset, primarily an educational settlement. Thus its first report of a year's activity begins with a page and a quarter on the work of its debating society—covering such subjects as " The Philosophy of Happiness ", " Empire Making by Chartered Company ", " The Educational Value of English ' Poetry ' and ' English Democracy ' "—and ends with four scant lines on District Visiting and ten on Summer Excursions.

If the range of the Settlement's early intellectual ambition seems, looking back on it from an age of educational expansion, prodigious, the response of the contemporary educational world is proportionately inspiriting. Owens College gave of its best, and from an awkward distance Oxford contributed its quota. In the first year, P. J. Hartog gave a University Extension course on Chemistry, and thereafter served Ancoats faithfully as tutor in English ; Dr. H. N. Alcock ran a class on ambulance work. A. W. Flux lectured on taxation, H. Rashdall on political philosophy, A. J. Carlyle on Carlyle and Ruskin, Edwin Cannan on Population. Professor Tout conducted a history class. In the course of the next few years Ancoats was instructed on philosophy and ethics by Samuel Alexander and A. E. Taylor ; on science by Professor Dixon ; on archaeology by Professor Boyd Dawkins ; on politics by J. J. Mallon and L. T. Hobhouse ; on economics by J. H. Clapham and Professor Gonner ; on Trade Unionism by J. R. Clynes ; on history by G. M. Trevelyan and Ramsay Muir. It is sometimes alleged—and indeed rightly—that the B.B.C. now brings to the remote and toiling masses of our community, the voices and thus some faint flavour of the personalities of the great men and women of our time. 'Thanks to the Settlement and Charles Rowley's Brotherhood, Ancoats had no need of the B.B.C. in this particular respect at the end of last century. It got its leading thinkers in the flesh—to see as well as to hear ; to talk to as well as to listen to.

Meanwhile, week by week through successive winter months the indefatigable regular workers of the Settlement : those who " spent *many* hours weekly there " as well as those who dwelt there, sustained their educational efforts with young and old alike. Mr. Pilkington Turner nursed the debating society week by week ; Mr. Edgar Worthington conducted a poetry reading group ; pupil teachers floundering between school and college were tutored in Latin, Literature, and Botany. Miss Stoehr, the pioneer resident, was the Settlement's botanist. Miss Eva Gore-Booth, later assisted by Miss Christabel Pankhurst and Miss Kemp, ran the " Ancoats Elizabethan Society ", so named in virtue of its intention to " revive a dramatic spirit, Elizabethan in the boldness of its aim and its independence of nineteenth-century machinery ". But for range of educational interest and persistence of educational enthusiasm during these early years a special meed of attention must be given to Miss Ellen Creak. Miss Creak taught young and old alike. To swollen classes of elementary school children she expounded the history of art. She was the exponent in Ancoats of Mazzini, St. Francis of Assisi, and the wonders of the sea. With a select group of adults she studied *Sophocles* in Plumtre's English verse translation, attempting by such study " to enter into the religious and ethical spirit of the plays, including the *Œdipus Rex* and part of the *Œdipus Coloneus* ". It is small wonder that one member of her group said, and others felt, that such reading had " opened up a new vista of thought ". Meanwhile, to those indisposed to leave their doorsteps and street corners on summer evenings in pursuit of art—art went forth as wooer under the leadership of Mr. and Mrs. Minton. Down into the courts and alleys of darkest Manchester and Salford trundled the Ancoats Hall piano, roped like the Ark of the Covenant to its swaying milk-float, surrounded by missionary musicians.

The response to Ancoats' need, of those who had intellectual light and learning to give, was certainly remarkable. " Freely thou hast received, freely give ", might have been the inspirational text of the University teachers and cultured middle-class women with time at their disposal who rallied to the Settlement during these earliest years. But, though some intellectual seeds will take root in virgin soil, it is as a rule thought necessary by cultivators to plough as well as to sow. And in so bleak a neighbourhood as Ancoats a good deal of ploughing had to accompany this intellectual

sowing. Education was, in fact, to an increasing degree
becoming entangled in those forms of social work familiar
to late Victorian and earlier Edwardian philanthropists, and
subsequently productive of much good grist for the mills of
legislative social reform. The earlier workers of the Art
Museum had already started the " ploughing " process by
their reception at Ancoats Hall of Elementary School children
for classes, concerts and 'dramatic entertainments. Their
work became merged in that of the Settlement—merged into
it and extended in all those directions familiar to volunteer
social workers in slum areas : readings to the blind, penny
banks, social evenings, dances, poor-man's lawyers, clubs
for boys, clubs for girls, clubs for the casual denizens of
common lodging houses, clubs for cripples ; and always,
everywhere, individual personal attention such as neighbours
give to neighbours for the remedy of their unclassifiable
misfortunes.

Unlabelled by Social Science Courses, unsustained by trust
funds or grants of public money, these Settlement workers
taught what they knew and learned as they taught. And
among them rose the darting flame-like personality of the
first woman Warden : Alice Crompton. Had one not known
for certain that she was a duly authenticated graduate of
Owens College, it might have been suspected that some
willowy pre-raphaelite lady, inflamed with an explosive
energy that was no part of her creator's ideal of feminine
grace, had burst suddenly out of an Art Museum folio, and
looping up dishevelled draperies, swept out into Ancoats to
find among its living people a warmth and variety of com-
panionship denied to the passive exhibits of the lecturer.

Many years later a Settlement worker of the nineteen-
thirties—knowing Professor Alexander's good repute as a
life-long feminist and an admirer of active intellectual women
—asked him what Alice Crompton was like, in those far off
Ancoats days. The old philosopher paused for a moment,
smiling with his eyes as though recapturing a pleasing visual
memory. Then—" She was a most beautiful creature," he
said.

CHAPTER IV

THE GOLDEN AGE

THE years 1902 to 1909, which cover the joint Wardenship of Alice Crompton and T. R. Marr, were for the Manchester Art Museum and University Settlement, a kind of golden age. It is true that they include the first worldwide cyclical depression of the new century, with 1904 recording a high peak of fragmentary unemployment percentages and initiating a dreary sequence of charitable funds for the relief of the destitute unemployed. But it is also true that the slow climb up from the trough of trade depression was enlivened, not as in the nineteen-thirties by the deadly stimulant of an armament programme, but by a series of important and expansive social reform measures. It was really during these first years of the new century that the philosophy underlying our acceptance of communal responsibility for social security became politically articulate and that the framework of our existing social security structure began to take shape. A realization that the edifice is still far from complete, should not obscure the fact that the Liberal Administration which held office first under Campbell Bannerman and later under Asquith, and which counted in its ranks an unusual array of individually distinguished men, accomplished a very significant feat of legislative pioneering. They inherited the Balfour Education Act of 1902, which gave us the administrative framework within which popular education could expand beyond the sixth standard of the elementary school. They also inherited the Unemployed Workmen Act of 1905, which gave faltering assent to the proposition that the State's responsibility for the unemployed does not begin and end with the offer of deterrent poor relief. And with this inheritance went a sitting Royal Commission on the Poor Laws, whose appointment was one of the last acts of Mr. Balfour's distintegrating ministry. This important bequest was in the nature of a delayed action bomb, timed to go off some two or three years later.

To this inheritance the new Liberal Government added with decent haste the Education (Provision of Meals) Act 1905 and the Education (Administrative Provisions) Act 1907, the first of which empowered education authorities to feed their children, while the second imposed the duty of medical inspection. There followed the Children's Act of 1908, which devised a host of new public sanctions for the protection of the young from parental negligence or exploitation. And in the same year came the Old Age Pensions Act of 1908, followed by an important double challenge to the *laissez faire* assumption that individuals can be trusted to make the most favourable disposal of their labour power, in the shape of the Labour Exchanges Act and the Trade Boards Act of 1909. By which time, with Winston Churchill in command of a brilliant administrative team at the Board of Trade and Lloyd George contemplating the possibilities of economic redistribution through Public Finance at the Exchequer, the stage was set for the culmination of this social reform programme in the National Health Insurance Act of 1911, coupled with its tentative advance into the unexplored field of unemployment insurance.

During most of these years the time-bomb, pending its explosion, continued to emit a thrilling tick. In other words, the Royal Commission on the Poor Laws, though sessions were prolonged until 1909, could not conceal the clash of social philosophies which divided its members into two camps and precipitated Majority and Minority Reports. From one camp, overlooking the Thames at Millbank, Mrs. Sidney Webb, the most brilliant and bellicose of the Commissioners, expounded the Webbian conception of communal responsibility, expressed through statutory machinery for a "national minimum" of material wellbeing. From an opposing camp in the Marylebone Road, Miss Octavia Hill inspired her rent collectors, fought her good fight for the preservation of open spaces, sustained the prudent scepticism of the Charity Organization Society, and week by week in the Committee Room of the Royal Commission upheld the cause of individual self-help against a rising tide of statutory provision.

There were few active social workers who did not at some point feel the throb of one or other of those power-houses of social endeavour. It gave to their smallest acts of neighbourly philanthropy as well as to their most imaginative efforts of pioneer reform, the dignity of logical integration with the laws of social science or human psychology. It added the salt of high politics and wide principle to the daily bread of social service. Looking back from an age tortured by doubt concerning the ability of civilization to survive, an age in which world war casts so long a shadow before that one can scarcely take pride in a building scheme without seeing it as a bomb target, it is difficult to recapture the exhilaration of these Edwardian years in the field of social service. Their ambitions may appear trivial measured by the actual or imagined achievements of planned national economies. Their material and cultural progress seems a little slow in view of the swift strides forward of which we now believe ourselves capable given the will backed by decisive manipulation of economic and political controls. But if they moved slowly, the reformers of those years at any rate moved forward—and with no thought of ever having to move back. They built without fear of destruction. The problems they encountered were big enough to awe and stimulate them, but not so big as to overawe them and belittle their varied tasks of personal service, experiment, and analysis. Those were indeed good years for social workers.

Up in Manchester, the Art Museum and University Settlement embarked upon its golden age with expanded equipment, and a new Constitution complete with Trustees. Its officers in this first year of joint existence were, in addition to its two wardens : Miss Crompton and Mr. Marr, a Curator (Mr. Thomas Collins), and an Assistant Secretary (Miss Beatrice Vernon). Its President was Mr. Horsfall, founder of the Art Museum ; its Hon. Warden, Alfred Hopkinson, Principal of Owens College. Its Hon. Secretaries were Mr. Pilkington Turner and Mr. Woodroofe

Fletcher; its Hon. Treasurer, John William Graham, Quaker Principal of Dalton Hall. But whatever social and political controversies stirred it, whatever its dusty pre-occupation with the health and housing, work and wages of its neighbours, its prime concern remained with mind and spirit. Thus first and foremost among its redefined objects stands the resolve : " to disseminate and nourish a healthy love of Nature and of the best in Art, Music, Literature, and Science ". Miss Octavia Hill would have said *Amen* to that. Mrs. Webb might have queried its priority.

But it was no mere pious resolve ; and indeed so rarefied was the Art and Education Committee's concept of its duty, that a minute of this early period records its refusal to house a newly discovered Roman coin on the ground that the proposed exhibit is " interesting from an antiquarian point of view rather than for its beauty ". It was in such an atmosphere of austere discrimination that Miss Creak moved on from Sophocles to an intensive study of the " Myth of Prometheus " ; and from there, carrying a class with an average attendance of 17·5, to Arnold's *Light of Asia* with readings from ancient Buddhist writings. In the following year, with an average attendance of 14, she concentrated on Browning's *Paracelsus*. " Ah, but a man's reach should exceed his grasp," or what's a Settlement for ? And if twenty-eight eager hands reached for *Paracelsus* they must have already grasped something of the *Light of Asia*, of Prometheus, and of Sophocles.

It is possible, of course, that the educational and cultural activities of the Manchester Art Museum and University Settlement benefited somewhat at this early period from the absence of the Palmerston Street Cinema within a stone's throw of its back door, and the Ardwick Empire within easy walking distance of its front. Indeed, the opening of the latter a few years later is mentioned in the minute book of the Art and Education Committee in connection with a slight decline of attendance at Settlement plays and concerts. It would, of course, take more than the absence of such competition to damp our astonishment at the prodigious intellectual and æsthetic reach of these early settlers. All the same—there *is* something in the Committee's tentative diagnosis. Social workers of this golden age enjoyed a local monopoly of cultural and recreative activities. Their principal competitor was the public-house. To-day they compete for their neighbours' leisure time with cinemas and dance halls ; with pin-tables and fun fairs and greyhound tracks ; with radio sets and the social amenities of Lewis's Stores. And the greatest of these is the cinema, because it at once stimulates the imagination, offers a response to the emotions, and provides a standard of technical perfection which no amateur effort can rival.

Meanwhile, the Settlement kept its feet on the ground and that ground was still the cobblestones of Ancoats. To judge from its reports during these years of Crompton-Marr dual control, its principal activities—though by no means all of them—other than the cultural, may be thus summarized:—

Prominent among all its recorded activities from year to year, and indeed one of its earliest ventures, is the Toynbee Debating Society, led by Mr. Pilkington Turner. It was there that the political and social problems of the day were argued out in the presence of large, and not exclusively Ancoats audiences. It was clearly a forum of some note— as a recorded average attendance of 65 for the session 1901–2 shows. The presence among its members of a good proportion of women was without doubt due to the activities of a sister organization : the Fawcett Debating Society for women, founded in 1900 with the object of challenging the supremacy of male self-expression which almost invariably manifests itself in mixed discussion groups. Never was uttered a more inaccurate cliché than that which credits women with volubility. In public, at any rate, they are the silent sex. But in nursing the Fawcett debating society to a healthy growth, Miss Crompton was markedly successful in redressing this balance. So much so, that six years after its inception it had seriously to consider a limitation on the length of speeches, in view of the growing " confidence " of its members.

Meanwhile, the more work-a-day forms of social endeavour grew and flourished. The Poor Man's Lawyer started by

J. W. Robson in 1898, swelled to a considerable panel of public-spirited men of law with a committee of its own, and in 1908 was reorganized with a card index system and more systematic arrangements for classification. A rise in the number of cases per evening session from 7 in 1901 to 60 in 1908 lies at the back of this development. The next step followed early in 1909, when the reorganized department called a conference of all the other Poor Man's Lawyer departments in Manchester and Salford, for the purpose of establishing as a uniform practice duly approved by the Manchester Incorporated Law Association, the regulations already in operation at the University Settlement. This purpose achieved, " a very enjoyable dinner " ensued.

A somewhat similar course was followed by the monthly parties for cripples, which were a very early feature of the Settlement's work. Two years after their inception Miss Crompton was inspired to avoid a somewhat depressing classification by adopting the name *Santa Fina*, in honour of the Italian girl saint, whose tale of physical suffering triumphantly borne is commemorated in the frescoes of San Gemignano. Thereafter they figure as *Santa Fina* parties, and their members as *Santa Finas*. From these periodic gatherings a considerable organization was in course of time evolved under the direction of Miss Helen Fisher, and by 1908 the *Santa Fina* work had become " a department in itself " with its own separate funds, its regular staff of visitors, its defined area, its systematic co-operation with other relevant organizations and agencies, and its careful accumulation of medical data. The 1902 Report refers to the need for such work in all poor localities, and expresses the hope that " in time this want will be met for the whole district by some organization which will include a wider area than the Association is able to cover ". That hope began to germinate in the following year with the formation of the Manchester and Salford Cripples Aid Federation. Its ultimate fine flower is the Invalid Children's Aid Association—one of the most important voluntary social agencies in the Manchester and Salford Area.

To the children of Ancoats, the Settlement made its own

peculiar contribution. Club work, which to-day is dignified, systematized, and subsidized as " the Service of Youth ", had drawn philanthropists to Ancoats before ever settlers settled there. Among their activities C. E. B. Russell's work at the Heyrod Street Lad's Club lies outside Settlement history and deserves a memoir of its own. But one small Settlement venture in this field may be mentioned not so much for its lasting effects as for its lack of them—against the kind of social background which makes a mock of charity. In a narrow street to the west of Ancoats and closely packed between its canals and factories, there stood a vast, ancient, and austere cotton mill. In 1892 this had been converted by a *tour-de-force* of architectural ingenuity into a vast honey-comb of 141 working class tenements under the name of Jersey Street Dwellings. Each tenement consisted of a kind of tunnel running from one side of the building to the other : a bedroom at one end, a living-room at the other, and between them a windowless " recess ", available as a minute second bedroom. Entrance was from a balcony, leading at the corner of each block, to outside staircases where com-munal w.c.'s were to be found. Each living-room was provided with a sink, a cold-water tap and a coalbunker. This repellent edifice represented, at the time with which we are here concerned, a philanthropic housing effort. How far the Company which promoted it was inspired by economic incentives it is now impossible to say. But the philanthropic element was certainly present, and something remotely suggestive of " Octavia Hill management " appears to have prevailed. Nearly half a century later, an inquisitive visitor, penetrating the gaunt and ravaged ruins of Jersey Street Dwellings, found among its few remaining inhabitants —since its tenancies, under Corporation pressure were not being renewed—an old woman who remembered the early years of the century with affectionate regret. She recalled a time when " the ladies " collected rents, brought flowers to the tenants and distributed coal. Pointing to a scene of dirt, disorder and fortuitous destruction in the yard, she deplored modern manners and the decay of parental control. But though, in addition to lack of parental control, all else round her spelt decay, she had no quarrel with the malodorous tenement which still contained her household gods ; and, indeed, found solid comfort in the fact that her windowless " recess " offered certain advantages as an air-raid shelter. To her visitor it was obvious that, with the eviction of the remaining tenants, the whole black towering shell of Jersey Street Dwellings would offer supreme advantages as an air-raid target. But even during its early years under semi-philanthropic management, the swarming youth of these Dwellings presented a social problem—and one which the Settlement made valiant attempts to solve. A single room, accorded to it, from 7 to 9.30 on six nights a week, by the Directors of the Dwellings Company, was used for a boys' club, which maintained a discouraging existence from 1898 to 1906. In that latter year the Dwellings changed hands ; and under new—and presumably hard-headed business-like —management, the existing social services were abandoned. With them went the Settlement's Club. Who knows what elements of grace it left behind it ? None, at any rate, that were subsequently perceptible to the human eye in Jersey Street Dwellings. There :

" . . . Penury, inertness and grimace,
In some strange sort, were the land's portion. ' See
Or shut your eyes,' said Nature peevishly,
' It nothing skills : I cannot help my case :
'Tis the Last Judgment's fire must cure this place,
Calcine its clods and set my prisoners free.' "

But to return to the Settlement's own children :—Under its new unified constitution the Art Museum, of course, continued its operations at full blast. To the elementary schools went its pictures and specimens. From the elementary schools came the children. And every Friday evening through every winter month 500–600 children came pouring in for a weekly entertainment of music, lantern pictures, or theatricals, as the case might be, organized by Miss Vernon. As long as any West End theatre queue and twenty times as talkative was the weekly crowd of waiting children, curved round the drive of Ancoats Hall, the fore-

most noses pressed against its door.   And as the years passed,
and with them Miss Vernon and the happy partnership of
Settlement and Museum, still they came : successive generations of Ancoats children, drawn by Miss Hindshaw's
" Children's Theatre ".   Neither cinema nor radio deflected
them from their allegiance, and on winter nights the dark
approach to Ancoats Hall echoed the anticipatory shuffling
of that waiting chattering throng, until the blackout of our
latter-day civilization imposed its menacing veto.

For older, but not yet wholly adult neighbours, Saturday
night dances in the great wooden Recreation Room in the
courtyard of 20 Every Street claimed a similar allegiance.
Their development provided the Settlement with a problem
requiring for its solution both firmness and tact.   Originally
these dances were not a Settlement activity at all, but a kindly
contribution to the amenities of Ancoats provided by an
earlier inhabitant of 20 Every Street—Mr. Francis Greg—
subject to an admission fee of 9d., and a mild degree of supervision by the caretaker of his playground and garden.   They
were popular but not always decorous—the less so as refreshment during the intervals of dancing was sought in neighbouring public-houses.   Even before the Every Street
property passed to the Settlement, Miss Crompton had been
invited by Mr. Greg to take over the supervision of these
dances, a task which she gladly undertook, paying over their
receipts to him each month.   As a result the dances, in the
opinion of Ancoats, became " a deal more respectabler than
they were ".   With the assumption of full ownership by the
Settlement in 1902, however, they became " more respectabler " still.   The " pass out " to public-houses was abolished
and refreshments (non-alcoholic) were supplied on the
premises.   The change brought regret to some of the wilder
spirits, but engendered a new confidence among anxious
mothers of daughters.   With which gain and loss the popu-
larity of the Saturday night dances was happily maintained.

For still older adherents of the Settlement the Field Club,
started in 1902, provided more sober occupation.   With the
fields a long way off and year by year retreating farther,
Field Club activities took its members on summer week-ends

over the hills and far away. From 60 in 1903, its membership swelled to a high peak of 152 in 1907. Abroad among
the hills it collected specimens ; at home among the houses
it mounted them for its herbarium. It bought plants and
bulbs in bulk and retailed them for cultivation in the
sulphurous atmosphere of Ancoats. It is significant, however, that " an outstanding feature " of its 1907 Flower
Show " was the awarding of 15 Aspidistras as prizes, the
Committee hoping that they might grow well in our sunless
corner of the town, and that the plants might be entered
for future shows ". Was this hope realized ? We do not
know. It is certain, however, that the aspidistra is a hardy
and enduring plant with the added advantage that its austere
foliage is washable, and we may surmise that the indomitable
fifteen, even if they failed to win prizes, long survived to
dignify if not to brighten Ancoats homes. It is, however,
regrettable that the report which records their appearance
has also to record " a little less interest taken in nature study,
with perhaps a tendency to develop into an open-air social
club ". With the passing of years this tendency became
more marked and the Field Club survived as an organization
for the enjoyment of golden memories and happy comradeship. As such it still survives.

One more among many social activities : the Tuesday " at
home " deserves to be recorded before we turn to the
development of Settlement policy which made all the others
possible and gave them abundant life. Like the children's
entertainment the Tuesday " at home " became an Ancoats
social habit, which in later years survived many ups and
downs of Settlement fortune. From small gatherings of
a dozen or so Ancoats neighbours meeting for talk, diversified
with music or recitation, these " at homes " grew in bulk till
their attendance reached three figures. But their informality
endured. Their participators remained unclassified either
by age, sex, or function. They were the friends who
dropped in.

And now for the backbone of these and many other
Settlement activities : the " fighting force " of the Settlement, to use the words of its 1904 Report ; or its " mainstay "

as described a year later. In 1899 it is recorded that " one
of the most interesting developments of the year " is the
formation of a body of Settlement Associates. All residents,
leaders of classes and members of the governing body were
ex officio Associates. To them were added by election any
persons who gave personal help to Settlement activities.
No subscription was demanded of them, but they maintained
a fund to which anonymous voluntary contributions might
be made. The 1902 Constitution gave them direct representation on the Council, and a year later we find them
holding monthly meetings to discuss plans with and make
suggestions to the Wardens, with J. J. Mallon and Teresa
Billington as joint secretaries. Mr. Pilkington Turner was,
and remained through thick and thin, a leader among them.
His enthusiasm for adult education stimulated them, his
kindness focussed their affections, and his courtliness set a
standard which came to be accepted in Ancoats as the perfect
pattern of what a University gentleman should be.

With the coming of the Associates the line between workers
and worked-among becomes blurred, and it is of the essence
of Settlement life that this should be so. Not that the
Associates were not workers. They were workers before
they were Associates. They worked to such effect as to
constitute themselves, by the systematic organization of
visiting, into what might now be called a " case work "
agency with a card catalogue, and in 1903 and 1904 their
visiting was directed—since these were pre-unemployment
insurance days—to finding out how many people in their
area were unemployed. But much of their energy was
focussed upon the development by co-operation of a full
civic and intellectual and æsthetic life amongst themselves.
It was the Associates who provided entertainment and
stewarding for the " at homes ". It was the Associates who
rented and ran a house at Carr Meadow Farm out on the
Derbyshire Hills, where they and their friends might enjoy
country holidays at cost price or secure meals in the intervals
of week-end rambles.

It is difficult, reading the printed records of those years,
to disentangle the Settlement from the Associates. But one

thing is made clear enough :—Like a star among them shone
J. J. Mallon, born leader, yet by an unusual natural combination, born co-operator. Let those who know J. J. Mallon
to-day, and who does not through one or other of his multifarious activities, imagine him in his exuberant youth. It
is easy enough, since the intervening years have not aged
or solemnized him, though they have landed him in exalted
company and attached a tail of significant letters to his name.
A Settlement contemporary of this early period has described
him as " the life and soul of every activity—bubbling over
with jokes, and breaking into humorous verse on every
occasion ". But though he gave off light and warmth to
those around him, one may perhaps think of him during
these years in Ancoats as an electric battery " on charge "—
accumulating human experience and generating vitality for
the larger part in this expansive era of social reform soon
to be demanded of him.

Not that the Settlement community in Ancoats failed to
reflect the optimism and respond to the stimuli of these
outside events. It did both. In its cultivation of æsthetic
values, in its dogged pursuit by road and rail of Nature's
wonders, in its preoccupation with Italian art and literature,
it reflected the ideals of Octavia Hill, disciple of Ruskin and
parent of the National Trust. But in its growing concern
for the development of the social services and its obvious
turn to the left in politics, it was incontestably Webbian.
This was probably due in large measure to the influence of
the Joint Warden, T. R. Marr, whose social politics shine
through the records of his multifarious cultural activities.
At any rate he was largely responsible for bringing Settlement
activities into close relation with Manchester municipal life
in which he played an active part ; and as Secretary of the
Manchester Citizens Association, under the Presidency of
T. C. Horsfall, he was responsible for producing in 1904
the survey of Housing Conditions in Manchester and Salford
mentioned on p. 9. This important monograph bears
strong traces of Booth and Rowntree influence and contains
bold suggestions for the expansion of municipal housing and
town-planning powers and for the rating of unoccupied land.

As early as 1899 Settlement workers had played their part in surveys of this kind, thus contributing grist to the mills of social legislation. But T. R. Marr undoubtedly brought the Settlement into closer touch with those developments of empirical economics which are a feature of this age of social reform. Not without cause was he known among his fellow-workers as " The Citizen ".

From another direction, too, great events vibrated in the air of Ancoats. The Women's Suffrage movement was emerging from its pioneering days and gathering momentum during this period. Manchester and London, running neck and neck, had, as early as 1866, shared the honour of producing the first two Suffrage organizations. Preponderantly a middle-class movement—since it is the middle-classes who have most time to examine the roots of their discontents and most leisure to grapple with them—in Manchester this characteristic was less marked than elsewhere. The connection between the economic servitude of women and their political impotence was duly noted, and it was from Manchester that many of the most active Women's Suffrage leaders came, especially those of them with trade union or Labour connections.

The impact of this movement on the Settlement in Ancoats was considerable. With some notable exceptions, among them Octavia Hill and Mrs. Humphry Ward, the restless social conscience which drove women into social work drove them also into the Suffrage movement. Octavia Hill's aloofness from the campaign was doubtless connected with her profound distrust of the legislative solution ; Mrs. Ward's active hostility was perhaps the product of a personal experience so rich in opportunity for the exercise of social and political influence that the vote could be written off as a crude, or at best a superfluous tool. To Alice Crompton and her fellow workers in Ancoats it was neither. It was the very basis of the wider democracy which patterned their work and coloured their personal contacts. Sweated female labour was carried on under their noses. Later, the Liberal Government, which so boldy demonstrated the possibilities of legislative action in the field of social reform, exasperated women by its obstinate negation in respect of a democratic franchise. It kindled the ambitions of the women social reformers, while it denied to them the tool whose uses were becoming increasingly obvious. To what extent the social services were drained of woman-power as the Suffrage movement gained momentum it is impossible to say. And it may be that such loss was later compensated by the intensive education in the processes of political democracy which the movement itself gave—at any rate to its constitutional adherents—before its final victory set them free to serve the cause of social reform and post-war reconstruction. But certain it is that many names of women prominent in the Women's Suffrage movement appear among the early workers at the Settlement and among those who came to speak to the people of Ancoats. Christabel Pankhurst, Teresa Billington, Mrs. Swanwick, Mrs. Despard, Eva Gore-Booth, I. O. Ford, Ellen Wilkinson, Eleanor Rathbone, Margaret Ashton—Ancoats saw and heard them all. True to its name, the Fawcett Debating Society flew the flag of feminism and carried its own banner in the Manchester Suffrage procession of October 24th, 1908. And its founder, Alice Crompton, was destined later to enrol under that flag, and march away from Settlement work with the armies of liberation.

One other strong external influence remains to be recorded : that of the *Manchester Guardian*. Throughout the whole history of the Settlement the *Manchester Guardian* has been an inspiration to its workers, a champion of its causes, and, incidentally, a vehicle to the outside public of its aims and needs. And its steady championship of Women's Suffrage at a time when that cause was not generally popular forged an additional link. But there were two other links which gave a peculiar personal intimacy to the relations between the Settlement and this great daily paper during the period with which we are concerned. The first was the presence among the Settlement's active workers of R. C. K. Ensor, who inhabited a neighbouring municipal dwelling at the time when he was a *Manchester Guardian* leader writer. His interest in the

Settlement was subsequently illuminated by his affection for one of its most active and faithful workers : Helen Fisher, whom he married in 1906.

The second was the presence among the men residents of Laurence Scott, eldest son of its editor, C. P. Scott, and his intended successor in the editorial chair. In a letter dated December 13th, 1903,[1] C. P. Scott wrote to his son, who had come down from Oxford with literary and artistic interests rather than a hereditary taste for politics : " For myself, I started in life with a very strong general feeling of devotion to humanity, and that helped me through and gave colour and interest to everything. You may get at the same sort of result, perhaps a better one, in other ways, building up from the particular instead of working down to it, if you will open yourself out. For I don't for a moment believe that real human sympathy, where it is called for, or a large and liberal interest in human affairs is in any degree lacking in you, only these things, like everything else that is good in us need exercise and nourishment. . . . When Ensor leaves you will have to take on the labour subjects, and it will take some hard work to prepare yourself. You must try and do some reading, and if you could get to know at first hand the way the poor live and the ways in which the very poor suffer it would no doubt help you very greatly. . . ." So Laurence Scott came to live in Ancoats. And there, the " real human sympathy " and the " large and liberal interest in human affairs " which were " in no degree lacking in him ", caused him to be much loved and long remembered by those amongst whom he worked. But it was left for others to reflect those qualities in the pages of the *Manchester Guardian*, for he died of tuberculosis in 1908.

All good times have an end, and Laurence Scott's untimely death was only one of many signposts pointing to the disintegration of the group of vivid personalities which transformed these middle years of the Edwardian era into a kind of golden age for the Settlement. Settlement work is, and always will be, intensely personal. It is an enterprise, to use C. P. Scott's phrase, " built up from the particular

[1] See *C. P. Scott*, by J. L. Hammond, p. 75.

instead of working down to it ", and the personal relationships of those engaged in it, their friendships and the
interplay of their contrasted and complementary qualities,
are the salt of its life. When fellow-workers go—or change—
the salt is apt to lose its savour. In 1906 Helen Fisher and
R. C. K. Ensor departed together as man and wife to take
up new work in London. J. J. Mallon was called away in
the same year to play a triumphant part in the campaign
for the Trade Boards Act, as Secretary to the Anti-Sweating
League. A year later Alice Crompton's home background
in Manchester had disintegrated and what with one thing
and another, ten years of life and labour lived with such
intensity seemed to be fairly rounded off. The Report,
for 1907–1908 foreshadows a change. It records growth :
" So many departments of work going that it is not easy to
keep all of them in close relation one with another." It
records activity in a wider field : in 1901 a Northern Settlements Federation, promoted by the Manchester Settlement
in 1901, came to roost for its seventh annual meeting in
Ancoats Hall, and the delegates found its deliberations " both
stimulating and fruitful ". There are new names among the
residents and workers, and two which were to prove later of
considerable significance to the Settlement : those of Emily
Jenkinson and Janet Blair. But there is another note.
" In recent years," say the Wardens, " some of our oldest
and most tried workers have gone off to other towns, and
the links formed by their personal friendships have been
to a large extent broken. . . . We have no fears for the
future. The time of transition will soon pass, and the places
of those old friends, whose loss we still regret, will soon be
taken by younger workers, to whom all that the Settlement
stands for will be as dear as it was to their predecessors."
The next report records the resignation of Alice Crompton
and T. R. Marr.

" History is lived forwards, but it is written in retrospect,"
writes an eminent historian. In retrospect we know that
the two retiring Wardens might well have " feared for the
future ", that the " time of transition " was prolonged to
the brink of disaster, and that it was very many years before

a group of Settlement workers was found to regenerate the zest of that golden age and inaugurate a new era of expansion. That the Settlement did in fact maintain a continuous existence until that time came, that those who were left carried on its work with dogged faith in its usefulness, and that others were found to serve it during its later years of eclipse, is due in a large measure to the live roots which the workers of the golden age had left in the soil of Ancoats. The sap continued to rise.

CHAPTER V

DIVORCE FROM THE ART MUSEUM

DURING the years which followed the break up of this vital family circle the Settlement lived on capital in more senses than one. In its figurative sense the process was not obvious to begin with, thanks to certain faithful helpers who kept up the pace and commanded the confidence of the Associates. Foremost among them stand Miss Emily Jenkinson and Miss Janet Blair. The pressure of their vitality held the sheet of Settlement activity taut, like the steady trade winds of the North Atlantic. Beyond their range lay the doldrums.

In February 1909 Mr. J. H. Whitehouse was appointed Warden. He came with a long record of social work at Ruskin College, at Bournville, and at Toynbee, but he had never encountered dirt of the quality and quantity which the atmosphere of Ancoats deposited upon Settlement property, and an introductory encounter with it horrified him. His first preoccupation was with the cleaning and reorganization of the Art Museum which had, under competitive pressure of Settlement social activities " of late years suffered no little neglect ". So much the Annual Report for 1909 admits. But his activities in this direction—as in all others so far as Ancoats was concerned—were short-lived. By the end of the year he was engulfed in national party politics. In January 1910 he entered Parliament, leaving his half-finished reorganization of the Art Museum to be completed " at the cost of much time and personal convenience " by the President, Mr. T. C. Horsfall, and the Hon. Treasurer, Mr. J. W. Graham. It was not until April 1911 that a full-time successor was appointed : Mr. G. V. Cox, formerly Co-Warden of Mansfield House Settlement in East London. For more than a year, therefore, the Settlement was without a Warden—or nominally so ; for in fact Miss Jenkinson, as head of the Women's House

of Residence, functioned as the quietly revolving hub of
Settlement activity. Emily Jenkinson was the most independent of mortals and the most unurbanized. Reared in
the West Highlands of Scotland, something of the brooding
silence of those highland country places had survived a spell
of London rent-collecting under the dictatorship of Miss
Octavia Hill. It has since survived other similar experiences ; and, reinforced by periods of living alone in the
company of dogs, remains to this day an element in her
personality. By virtue of it, she is able to exert an authority
over unruly children out of all proportion to her physical
stature and the volume of her voice. Being thus capable of
working alone, she was not during this period required to
do so, having the support of Miss Janet Blair, the Secretary
of the Santa Fina Committee. Nevertheless, the 1910
Report records a marking of time in consequence of the
interregnum between Wardens. " Less has been attempted "
we are told. And the Toynbee Debating Society reports
a diminution of numbers as a result of which its secretary
resigned. The 1912 Report records its last appearance,
with a note regretting a general falling off of interest. The
same Report complains of a " lack of enthusiasm at present
noticeable in many of the Visitors ", some of whom " appar-
ently do not distribute concert tickets and do not attend the
concerts, a valuable means of getting into closer touch with
those whom they visit ". In the Fawcett Debating Society,
however, attendance was well maintained, and among the
subjects expounded to its members was the Minority Report
of the Poor Law Commission, which reminds us that Mr.
and Mrs. Webb's whirlwind campaign for the " Break up of
the Poor Law " was the dominant social controversy of the
time. There seems to have been no one in these regions
to expound the compromise proposals of the Majority Report.

So Mr. Cox comes on the scene, and Miss Jenkinson
retires from it—until her return many years later to perform
a new difficult task on the Settlement's behalf. And the
1911 Report which records Mr. Cox's name as Warden,
records at the same time the appointment of a new Hon.
Officer : Mr. George St. C. Robertson as Secretary. From

that day to this Mr. Robertson's name has figured in that same office, sometimes alone, sometimes with a collaborator, under successive wardens, through three major Settlement crises, two world wars and a great trade depression—always there. At no point in the Settlement's long drama has Mr. Robertson taken the stage, asserted his personality, or imposed his opinion. One sees him always as a constant, slightly stooping figure, with a peculiarly gentle smile, standing just outside the circle of limelight. One is apt to take his unobtrusive helpfulness for granted as one takes for granted the unchanging affection of a near relative. But in 1944 his colleagues woke up to the fact that for thirty-five years this help had been steadily forthcoming, and they chose to express their recognition of the fact by the ceremonious presentation to him of four volumes. Among them was William Temple's *Readings in St. John's Gospel* : a singularly appropriate gift, though in one respect an unnecessary one, since the recipient's whole life had reflected in his dealings with his fellow-men and his forgetfulness of self, a perfect understanding of the gospel of that beloved apostle.

But to return to the starting-point of this thrust into a later age. In respect of the Wardenship, the Settlement's luck continued to be badly out of joint. G. V. Cox brought valuable experience to the work in Ancoats and a certain romantic charm of personality, but it was not, unfortunately, accompanied by robust health. Within a year it was decided that he must absent himself from its rigours for part of the year. In May 1913 even this partial release, assisted by the presence of a sub-warden, proved too great a strain, and he resigned, to be succeeded in the following month by Mr. G. K. Grierson, formerly Secretary to the Salford Civic League of Help. It was left to Mr. Grierson to pilot the Settlement into the dark waters of the First World War.

But neither Mr. Grierson's advent, nor the continued vitality of the Fawcett Debating Society, nor the adhesion of the Associates, nor the continued weekly gathering of the Tuesday " at homes " could recreate the indefinable social cohesion of the Crompton-Marr régime. Something had gone out of the Settlement and those who loved it were beginning to look backwards. The force generated at the centre by " high powered personalities " was spending itself. But that is only part of the story. It is probable that the Settlement had suffered the fate which sometimes overtakes nations when their colonizing reach exceeds their imperialist grasp. It is a fate which may be fraught with good results for humanity in the long run, but disappointing results for national self-esteem in the short run. The Settlement was, in fact, colonizing in the field of social service over a wider area and outside the family circle. And the result of this process, though conducive to the historical repute of the Settlement, to the furtherance of its social ideals, and to the well-being of its parent City, had immediately devitalizing effects upon its internal social structure. On a wide view the game was worth the candle but there was some danger of the candle going out.

Let us, then, observe the operation of this process on a few of the Settlement's major activities. It was, in fact, a double process. Some of the Settlement's work moved out of the circle and became merged in that of outside organizations. Some of the work of outside organizations moved into the circle and was carried on there in the name of the larger specialist body.

In 1909, for example, the personal " case-work " of the Settlement, operated very largely by Settlement workers, began to function as the Ancoats District (A.3) of the City League of Help. The Ancoats Hall Poor Man's Lawyer had, as we have seen, already developed on these lines as one local branch of a large regional organization.

Ancoats' educational activities had certainly declined since the age of Sophocles and Paracelsus. But in 1911, at the invitation of the Warden, the Workers' Educational Association adopted Ancoats Hall as a local centre for its classes, thus bringing Ancoats students into relation with a national educational crusade which had not existed at the time of the Settlement's inception. It may be that Ancoats intellects were the better prepared for an adequate response because of what the pioneer Settlers had set stirring in them. But of this there is no direct evidence.

Among the children, too, new outside allegiances were being formed, and Ancoats troops of Boy Scouts and Girl Guides, of Cubs and Brownies, arose to take their place in a world-wide movement. But it was not until 1918 that the Fawcett Debating Society merged its identity in that of the Manchester and Salford Women Citizens' Association, whose New Cross Branch it eventually became.

Perhaps the most constructive and spectacular of these integrating processes was that which eventually transformed the Santa Fina Society, the evolution of which into a branch of the Invalid Children's Aid Association has already been foreshadowed.

In 1910 the Santa Fina Society, already in possession of its own separate accounts, appears with its own separate committee membership on the title page of the Annual Report, with Miss Janet Blair as its Secretary and Mr. G. St. C. Robertson as its Hon. Treasurer. It is here described for the first time as a " Branch of the Manchester Art Museum and University Settlement ". In the following year's Report its work is briefly summarized with reference to a full report published separately. But the summary also refers to the Committee's proposal to start a special Cripples' School for those unfit to attend the Elementary Schools. This school was duly opened at the Settlement in October 1911, with 12 children. By the following April there were 40 children on the register with an average attendance of 30, and Miss Blair is able to report that the general improvement in the health and intelligence of the children is so satisfactory as fully to justify the experiment. The final stage of its swift evolution from voluntary experiment to statutory provision is described as follows in the Settlement's Annual Report for the year ending April 1913 :—

" The Settlement Council have much pleasure in recording the progress of the Cripple Day School. When the school opened there was no provision in the city for the daily education of children excluded from the elementary schools by reason of their infirmities. The Manchester Education Committee have now realized the value of the work, and from June 1st of this year took over the school as one of their special schools. The initiation of this work is a piece of pioneer work with which the Settlement and especially the Santa Fina Society may well feel deep satisfaction. It is a matter for just pride that a municipal activity which is bound to be of increasing importance was started through our realization of the need and an activity in showing how the remedy could be applied."

The same Report refers to the extension of the Santa Fina work on the preventive side to provide for the care and supervision of invalid children—a change of scope which precipitates a change of name. From now on the Santa Fina Committee dissolves into the Manchester Invalid Children's Aid Association whose reports must be sought elsewhere than among the archives of the Settlement. Thus, poor little Santa Fina may be left to suffer through the ages in her San Gemignano frescoes—unless the destructive fury of the Germans has by now obliterated them. In Manchester the forces of preventive medicine, surgery and social science are mobilized to preserve her kind from sanctified suffering and untimely death.

This job accomplished, Miss Blair submitted herself to a comparable process of integration with the wider activities of her city. In April 1914 she married Mr. W. H. Zimmern, thus joining forces with a family already well known in the civic life of Manchester, to whose beneficent activities she has since added many more of her own. Her place as Secretary of the I.C.A. Association and Head of the Women's House at the Settlement was taken by Miss Nora Teale, and the work of the I.C.A.A. went steadily and expansively forward.

One other branch of Settlement activity in a larger field must be mentioned before turning to the advent of a new and significant force in Ancoats—since it typifies the part that Settlements were beginning to play and were indeed destined to play with increasing significance as time went on : the collection and sifting of information in the cause of social science. Under the inspiration of T. R. Marr, Settlement workers had accumulated unemployment statistics among the unskilled and largely unorganized wage-earners of Ancoats, in the days before the machinery of unemployment insurance produced comprehensive unemployment percentages as a by-product of social security. And Ancoats workers had played their part in his well-documented survey of Manchester and Salford housing conditions. In November 1909 the Poor Man's Lawyer Department put its own machinery to similar use by suggesting to the Royal Commission then occupied with the problems of Divorce and Matrimonial Causes, that the Department might be in a position to give valuable evidence from the working-class standpoint. The suggestion was welcomed and the Department set to work. Seven hundred and fifty matrimonial and bastardy cases were disinterred and their applicants invited to retell their stories. A hundred and ninety responded to the invitation, and a mass of evidence, together with certain conclusions arising therefrom, were presented in person to the Commission by the Hon. Secretary of the Department. Later, on the eve of the war, when the ties between the Settlement and the University were strengthened by the fact that Mr. Grierson, the Warden of the Settlement, held a lectureship in Social Science at the University, the Settlement workers were mobilized to collect material from the whole Manchester district for the investigation which the Raten Tata Foundation at the London School of Economics was making into the working of the Trade Boards Act of 1909. The Settlement was, indeed, growing increasingly Social Science minded. It was, in this respect, following in the footsteps of Toynbee Hall. Charles Booth had, of course, shown what could be done with a mass of recorded individual experience in the early 'nineties.

The Settlement was growing increasingly Social Science minded. What, then, of the Art Museum, with its Art and Education Committee which in days gone by had spurned a Roman Coin because it was not beautiful ?

We have already noted Mr. Whitehouse's truncated effort to atone for a period of " no little neglect " of the museum and its contents. Mr. Horsfall and Mr. Graham did their best to finish his work of rehabilitation, but it is clear that

E

though the rooms and corridors of Ancoats Hall echoed to
the tramp of busy feet, the pictures which adorned its walls,
the exhibits which occupied its show cases, were not getting
the affectionate attention they deserved and had at one time
commanded. It is not surprising, therefore, that in the
autumn of 1912 the Art and Education Committee found
itself discussing the possibility of appointing a permanent
curator. " Such a person," said Mr. Graham, " should be
refined and educated, and since it was impossible to get such
a man at the salary the Settlement could offer, it must
necessarily be a woman." Two months later Miss Bertha
Hindshaw was appointed at a salary of £50 a year to act as
Assistant Curator from 3 to 9 p.m. each day. That the Art
Museum had secured at very moderate cost an officer of
" refinement and education " was apparent from the start.
As time went on, it became obvious that they had secured
much else. They had, in fact, secured the lifelong devotion
of a single-minded enthusiast. Within a year " her reorganization of the pictures had added very greatly to their value
and usefulness, and her talks to classes of school-children
and to the children of the district who flocked on Sundays to
her informal conversations were of real moment as a part
of the Settlement's efforts to spread in Ancoats the sense
and love of beauty ". Within two years it became apparent
that the social activities of the Settlement and the cultural
activities of the Art Museum were in hot competition and
treading on one another's toes. One thing Miss Hindshaw
would not stand, and that was the casual removal of Art
Museum material for Settlement purposes. She could, in
fact, assume the aspect of a tigress in defence of her young ;
and if anything was to suffer " no small neglect " it was not
going to be the Art Museum this time. Working together—
lunching together—Miss Hindshaw, by now full-fledged
Curator of the Museum and Mr. Grierson, Warden of the
Settlement, lived a life which may be compared with the
" Holy Deadlock " experienced by the hero and heroine of
A. P. Herbert's novel. Each longed for disentanglement
from the other's work, while the Art and Education Committee sought for reasonable grounds of divorce.

The war years with their inevitable frustration of Settlement activities brought release from this uncomfortable situation. In May 1917 a special meeting of the Art and Education Committee was held to consider the conditions of separation. Councillor Todd, Chairman of the Manchester Corporation Art Committee, was present at the meeting. The Corporation was, it seems, prepared to consider the incorporation of the Museum in the system of Municipal Art Galleries. What of the Settlement? Mr. Graham confessed that " much of the Settlement was going anyhow ", and the group of rooms in the north wing previously used as the Women's House could be used for Settlement purposes—there was still 20 Every Street for the women residents. On these terms the separation was arranged. On July 19th, 1918, the Art and Education Committee held its last meeting, and the Report for that year was the last to bear the combined title " Manchester Art Museum and University Settlement ". Barriers were erected one above the other in each of the three long corridors of Ancoats Hall, barring the north wing from the main building. There was to be no more predatory commandeering of museum exhibits for Settlement purposes, no more competitive claims on the attention of the same committees or the energies of the same workers. And what are we going to do with you? said Councillor Todd to Miss Hindshaw. Miss Hindshaw replied that she was one of the Museum's Exhibits. This was an understatement. She was, in fact, its driving force, its champion, its mistress and its servant. As such she went with it, merely transferring her services from the Settlement to the City ; a side-step from the Third to the Second Bureaucracy.

The barriers in the Ancoats Hall corridors, erected in 1918, remain to-day precisely as they were, and on her own side of them Miss Hindshaw rules supreme among the crowds of children who still flock to what is now the City's Horsfall Art Museum. Her attitude to the Settlement has moved from militant hostility to non-belligerency—from non-belligerency to armed neutrality To-day her neutrality is not untinged with benevolence. But it is still armed.

And now to return to the main stream of our tale, the

fortunes of the Settlement itself. Mr. Graham's admission, recorded in the Art and Education Committee's minutes of May 1917, that " much of the Settlement was going anyhow ", needs further explanation, of which the date itself provides some part. The first world war hit the Settlement work hard. Its opening phase, with the threat of incalculable industrial dislocation—since we had not then learned the uses of war as an instrument of full employment—demanded the mobilization of all the Settlement's available forces as a relief agency. The Art Museum became the Divisional Office for relief in the Ancoats district and the Warden assumed the duties of Divisional Secretary. Work centred mainly on the needs and problems of the soldier's wife. There was, of course, no statutory authority comparable with the present-day Assistance Board to bear the brunt of it.

New demands for systematic enquiry also presented themselves, and in the first year of war a group of Settlement workers, including about thirty University students, carried on an investigation into the effect of rising prices on working-class households, the results of which were transmitted by Professor Chapman to the Local Government Board. All of which meant more work for the Settlement rather than less, and to begin with, many volunteers were forthcoming. But the men residents had melted away and 20 Every Street was functioning as the private residence of the Warden. The social life of the Settlement thus lost the old vitalizing element once described by Mr. Horsfall as " co-occupation ".

Meanwhile, the second year of war produced what the Report for 1916 describes as " a disturbing feature ". The effects of mental strain were making themselves felt in Ancoats. The women, far from suffering from the expected unemployment, were suffering from long working hours against a background of family separation. " Amongst the young people an increase in displays of nervous excitement " was perceptible. And " a marked change for the worse was taking place in the conduct of the children ". It was observed that " the previous minor misdeeds of a few boys were now the regular practices of large groups ". To meet these ugly tendencies and " prevent the school holidays from aggravating this condition ", the Settlement maintained a holiday centre for a hundred Ancoats children throughout August 1915. It involved visits to private gardens round Manchester and excursions far into the country, and proved to be the forerunner of an annual activity continued into years of peace. In co-operation with Miss Teale of the Invalid Children's Aid Association and with the friendly help of the School Medical Officer, the first School Care Committee in Manchester was organized. And during the winter a children's play centre was established at the Settlement. These efforts were not unnoticed by the Board of Education and led to an official recommendation in favour of the organization of play centres by local education authorities. So far so good.

But the Settlement was, as the opening words of this chapter suggest, living on capital, and for an accurate apprehension of this process we must turn to its financial history.

In 1908 a serious curtailment of work, owing to financial stringency, was averted by a timely bequest of £2,000 from Mrs. Rylands. Of this, £281 was used to meet a deficit on the 1909 year's working, and the rest invested in Sheffield Corporation Stock. Meanwhile, the Hon. Treasurer, Mr. J. W. Graham, appealed for an additional annual income of £400 to meet such deficits in future. Unhappily, it was not forthcoming. In 1910 a similar deficit occurred and some of the newly purchased stock was sold to meet it—a process which was repeated in the following year. In 1912 the deficit had fallen to £85, thanks partly to the absence of any unusual item of heavy expenditure, and partly to Miss Blair's business-like management of the residents' housekeeping which, in the absence of overhead charges for rent, yielded a profit of £74. But in 1913, despite a housekeeping profit of £213, the deficit had risen to £270. All Miss Blair's financial skill had failed to keep the wolf from the door. Once again an inroad was made on the Rylands bequest and once again Mr. Graham uttered his appeal for an increased regular income—but all to no avail. In 1914 the deficit rose to £360 and the Rylands bequest was almost exhausted. In 1915 it *was* exhausted. An attempt to reduce current expenses by handing over the Every Street garden and playground to the Corporation Parks Committee was unsuccessful, and the Settlement was brought face to face with the ugly prospect of having to sell the Every Street property so joyfully acquired in 1902. This desperate situation was saved by a *Manchester Guardian* appeal to the public, which produced £365 in donations to meet a further deficit of £242. But these were unfortunately donations—not subscriptions ; and Miss Blair's hand was no longer on the tiller of Settlement housekeeping which under pressure of rising war prices showed a loss of £36. In 1917, for the first time in the Settlement's history, current income and current expenditure balanced. This result is explained by Mr. Graham as being due partly to great economy and the receipt of special donations, partly, however, to a more sinister cause : the postponement of repairs.

It was at this point, in September 1917, that Miss Beatrice B. Rogers was appointed as Warden of the Settlement in succession to Mr. Grierson, who left to join the Navy at Whitsuntide of the same year. She entered into a bleak heritage.

CHAPTER VI

THE SETTLEMENT'S CRISIS

MISS ROGERS entered upon her bleak heritage in September 1917, but the complete picture of its bleakness was not at that date fully revealed. The war situation was discouraging and there seemed no predictable end to it. Manners and morals in Ancoats were on the down grade, but the post-war trade depression with its spectacular unemployment percentages, its weary reaction from the "homes for heroes" mood, and its orgy of uncovenanted benefits, was yet to come. This last development may have preserved the people of Ancoats from the bare-footed beggary familiar to Victorian philanthropists. It did not, however, preserve them from the state of dreary destitution, on whose precarious edge the bulk of them habitually lived. Against a background of external discouragement and local demoralization, Miss Rogers stepped into premises whose current repairs had been indefinitely postponed and whose main building was about to be removed from her jurisdiction by an implacable secessionist.

In one respect she was well fitted to meet this situation. She was accustomed to be poor among the poor. She did not care what she ate or where she slept or how she dressed, and was mildly puzzled by the attitude of those who did. She had no careerist ambitions. She was completely selfless. Looking out upon the world through powerful round spectacles she was able to see the Kingdom of Heaven not very far away. She could not, however, see the chaos on her writing-table nor the objects which she had borrowed from the museum and subsequently mislaid. And in this respect she was not well-fitted for her new task. Her ministry was an added exasperation to Miss Hindshaw; her disdain of creature comfort a deterrent to potential residents. Her first big job, therefore, the disentanglement of the Settlement from the Art Museum on the terms agreed by the Council of the Settlement and the municipal authorities, encountered no aftermath of reluctance on the Art Museum side, and was driven through with all dispatch. The decree was made absolute—in other words, the separation was confirmed—at the Annual Meeting in June 1919, on which occasion the Manchester University Settlement assumed its present name. At the Annual Meeting in December of the following year a new simplified Constitution was adopted and the occasion was marked by the resignation of Mr. Horsfall from the Presidency, an office which he had held from the date of the Settlement's inception. It was a very natural move on his part. He was in his eightieth year and his first love had always been the Museum, which to-day bears his name. But he had been a good friend to the Settlement, and his resignation emphasized its break with the past. He was succeeded by Sir Henry Miers, Vice-Chancellor of the University of Manchester which had developed out of Owens College.

Two other breaks with the past remain to be noted. In 1919 Mr. J. W. Graham fell ill and resigned the Hon. Treasurership after his long heroic struggle with debit balances, bequeathing to his successor an overdraft of £143. And in the same year Miss Teale removed the office of the now independent Invalid Children's Aid Association from Settlement premises to new premises in the centre of Manchester, leaving behind her as an enduring Settlement activity, the Disabled Folks' Guild.

And so Miss Rogers, set to work. The last ferocious onslaught of the war came—and passed—in a turmoil of Armistice rejoicings and the sudden cessation of war casualties merging into the most ferocious influenza epidemic within memory. In Ancoats it necessitated the closing of the schools, which did not assist the return of juvenile law and order. But the new Warden was able to use the blessed word " reconstruction " in her first report, calling upon the University and the Settlement " to scan the horizon, to rally the scattered workers, to give a lead to generous youth, to make the demands of peaceful Reconstruction and social service as appealing and as irresistible as those of national military service ". And for the first time the usefulness of the Settlement as a training centre was emphasized. A year later she was able to cite the reorganization of a Social Study course at the University as an incentive to Settlement effort, and draw attention to the wider contribution which University Settlements were making, and should be expected to make, in co-operation with Universities, to the development of Social Science. It will be remembered that the years following the first world war were notable for a considerable volume of constructive work on these lines, culminating in the formation of the Joint Universities Council for Social Studies, and for a growing consciousness of the value of systematic training under University auspices, for the jobs opened up by an increasing range of social services both statutory and non-statutory. The Third Bureaucracy was expanding rapidly and the Settlements were called upon to provide much of the clinical training for its certificated members. Miss Rogers was not unaware of this important trend of events, and one of her earliest activities was the organization of a group for the study of post-war industrial problems.

But there is a new note in Settlement activities that is distinctively Rogers : the development of Settlement contacts with working-class, as distinct from philanthropic organizations. With the Workers' Educational Association contact had already been made. Miss Rogers pushed it further. With the National Union of Railwaymen, whose Ancoats membership was pretty considerable owing to the large area occupied by Railway Co. warehouses, goods yards and stables, she developed from 1921 onwards, very close contacts, both educational and social. A N.U.R. Education Committee was the result of her efforts. There was a further result in May 1926 when, on the eve of the great general strike of that year the local branch of the N.U.R. crowded into the Recreation Room, some hundreds of excited, anxious, apprehensive trade unionists, to discuss their policy in regard to it. Never was a less revolutionary gathering. Never were. Britons, entering upon a struggle whose end could not be foretold, whose risks could not be defined, more conscious of their grave responsibility in responding to the call of their leaders. Never were the workers of this country more firmly determined that if violence were to result, it should be none of their making. It was a gathering which will long remain in the memory of those who attended it and from which social science students, had they been present, might have learned much about the character of British trade unionism. When it broke up at midnight, Miss Rogers and a few of her helpers adjourned to the North Wing of Ancoats Hall to establish a head-quarters and refreshment centre for the pickets going out in relays through the dawn. It was unfortunate that Ancoats Hall happened to be Railway Co. property in occupation of the Corporation Art Galleries Committee by whom Miss Rogers was subsequently called angrily to account for her partisanship in an industrial dispute. Nevertheless, there is some satisfaction in the thought that it was to the Settlement that the workers of Ancoats turned at a moment of grave anxiety, and that the Settlement, flinging politic prudence to the winds, responded readily with sympathy and soup.

Meanwhile, normal Settlement activities went forward in the teeth of ever-deepening post-war trade depression. The Tuesday " at homes " had triumphantly survived the war, though with the loss of the larger rooms at Ancoats Hall their accommodation presented difficulties. The Recreation Room was too cold and draughty for social amenity. But a certain measure of cold comfort could be achieved by the use of a smaller room inset in its gaunt interior. The Field Club continued to meet and ramble. The cottage at Hayfield had failed to survive, but the open country, though driven further away by the expansion of Manchester post-war housing, was still accessible. A children's dancing class conducted by Miss Bateman, under the auspices of Miss Madge Atkinson's school of dancing, had become a regular feature of Settlement life, and provided the prettiest sight in Ancoats. But the most important development of the immediate post-war period was the elaboration of the children's Summer holiday school with its separate finances and its paid superintendent. From 1920 onwards the children of Ancoats were wafted by tramcar every day during the Summer holiday to the outskirts of Manchester, there to be entertained, in elementary school premises lent by the Education Committee, to activities as unlike the normal school routine as the Superintendent and a band of amateur helpers could make them. The air of Didsbury could not challenge that of Blackpool; it was, however, incomparably less sulphurous than that of Ancoats.

But as the whole country ran into the dislocations of post-war trade depression a cloud settled upon Ancoats which was not destined to lift until the second great post-war depression had run its course. Long term unemployment became a feature of the district. The relief of distress became a leading Settlement activity and a major preoccupation of its Warden. In report after report from 1921 onwards we are made aware of this. Since the end of the war—and, indeed, since the beginning of her reign as Warden—Miss Rogers had devoted a deal of energy to what is technically called " case work ", but which may be otherwise described as the piloting of ill-educated or ill-informed individuals through their personal entanglements. During the difficult transition period 1918–19 the report of the Poor Man's Lawyer makes special mention of her services as Divisional Representative of the National Relief Fund in connection with the handling of pensions and gratuity cases. Then in the winter of 1920–1 mass unemployment began to make itself felt. In the country at large, the unemployment percentage, by now accurately gauged by the machinery of the 1920 Act which extended national unemployment insurance to practically the whole range of industrial and commercial wage-earning, rose from 11 per cent. in January 1921 to a high peak of 23 per cent. in May of that year. In Ancoats the Report for 1920–1 records that " appeals for advice by people almost overcome by difficulty and discouragement due to unemployment in the neighbourhood are far greater than in any previous winter ". The Warden met it in various ways. Every morning she constituted herself into an enquiry office. In January and February 1922 no less than 400 applicants for help and counsel visited her.   Meanwhile, a clothing club was instituted to meet the needs of the families of unemployed men for whom insurance and extended benefits—not to mention outdoor poor relief allowances—allowed no economic margin for replacements. Cast-off clothing was appealed for ; an out-of-work woman was kept busy with its reconditioning.   From an emergency fund partly raised by the sale of such clothing, relief grants were made in selected cases. The Settlement, which was never intended to function as a relief agency, under pressure of circumstances was rapidly moving in that direction. And outside organizations assisted the process.   A Lord Mayor's Fund for the provision of dinners for expectant and nursing mothers used the Recreation Room as one of its centres. That gaunt and comfortless edifice served also as one of the Lord Mayor's Social Centres for Unemployed Men.   Its need of redecoration, re-equipment and repair became increasingly urgent under the pressure of those slopping plates, those irresponsible shuffling feet.   Year after year there are complaints of uncovered wear and tear ; but the necessary funds for its renovation were not forthcoming.

Indeed, for none of these pressing activities were the necessary funds forthcoming. We have seen that Mr. Graham's heroic struggle as Hon. Treasurer ended in 1919 with an overdraft of £143.   In the following year a legacy of £150 from Miss Gaskell—the Settlement's last link, through her daughter, with the author of *Cranford*—saved an awkward situation and the debit on the year's working was only £16.   But outside the General Fund, to which these figures relate, a growing number of special funds balanced satisfactorily, and the Settlement was in fact administering an income of over £2,000 a year, in which for the first time a Board of Education grant of £19 17s. 6d. for the play centres was a significant item.   It was the forerunner of later and larger grants of public money for similar purposes and a sign of the time, fast approaching, when all over the country, non-statutory bodies would act in partnership with central and local government organs for the administration of popularly approved social services. Meanwhile, the

General Fund languished. In 1921 it just paid its way—and again in 1922, thanks to a special donation of £200. But in 1924 the deficit rose to £181 2s. 5d. and in 1925 the Settlement could not afford to publish an Annual Report.

These figures make it quite clear that the Settlement, like its neighbours, was struggling with poverty. And there was no longer a Miss Blair or a Miss Jenkinson to keep the residents' house in order. Miss Rogers was no adequate substitute. Household management was not her strong suit. She did not regard it as important. When the founders of the Settlement pledged its settlers to lead " a simple and religious life " among their neighbours, they can have had no conception of the degree of simplicity to which religious devotion would impel Miss Rogers. It became increasingly difficult to find any one to share it with her. In 1918–19, nine residents occupied 20 Every Street for varying periods of time—in several cases less than a month—and six holiday school-helpers, including four teacher trainees from Bingley Training College, lodged there during August. In the following year only five fleeting occupants experienced the rigours of the Every Street *ménage*. Thereafter there is no record of residents. Miss Rogers herself occupied a room whose internal structure included a pipe which continually sneezed and gurgled on its way to and from an awkwardly placed attic lavatory. She appeared to be perfectly contented with it. In October 1923 three experienced and business-like female members of the Council were appointed as a sub-committee on the domestic arrangements of 20 Every Street. Their efforts ran aground on its discomforts.

It is probable that these discomforts had something to do with the failure of successive efforts made by the Council to secure permanent paid help for Miss Rogers. In 1923 an advertisement for an assistant Warden (male or female) produced only unsuitable candidates. An alternative effort to secure a half-time secretary for the Warden at £5 a month plus lunches was more successful, but the success was ephemeral, and a series of such appointments followed by resignations are recorded in the Council minutes. A proposal by Miss Rogers that financial stringency be met by a reduction of her own salary found no favour with the Council, but it may be surmised that she found ways of her own to evade this official veto. Meanwhile, her day-to-day ministry in Ancoats was increasingly prejudiced by the necessity of conducting money-raising propaganda meetings over a wide area. A minor alleviation was finally achieved in 1924 when, after long correspondence culminating in a threat of legal proceedings, a tenant who had for some time rented the Round Chapel for industrial purposes was induced to pay arrears of rent and clear out—leaving a general disorder of sawdust and woodshavings behind him.

At this stage there can be little doubt that the University was growing heartily tired of its Settlement, and not without cause. Month by month its patient and genial Vice-Chancellor, Sir Henry Miers, presided at Council meetings whose main business seemed to be grappling with financial crises and salvaging derelict premises. Professor Macgregor made a brief effort as Hon. Treasurer. Professor Chapman undertook to canvass the University staff. But on a superficial view the Settlement had not the inspiriting appearance of a going concern. It is not surprising, therefore, that a new idea began to take sinister shape, the idea, that if Settlement property could not be maintained in good order it had better be dispensed with altogether. Once before at a crisis of Settlement history the sale of the Every Street property had been proposed and averted. Now, a proposal having very similar implications began once more to stir in the minds of the Council.

In October 1923 the question was raised : should further money be spent on the disintegrating Recreation Room ? Professor Dickie, Professor of Architecture in Manchester University, was invited to report on the cost of restoring it to decent order. A month later he presented a report both on the Recreation Room and the Round Chapel. The figures were intimidating, and a sub-committee was appointed to consider them ; together with the uses to which the premises in question ought to be put—and possible sources of income to be extracted from them. From its deliberations emerged the view that the most useful part of the Round Chapel was its site, and that this might, with advantage to all concerned, be offered to the Manchester Education Committee for the erection of a nursery school. Negotiations dragged on, but the Manchester Education Committee was not enthusiastic. There were certain difficulties. The land immediately surrounding the Round Chapel was paved with tombstones beneath which the remains of Dr. Scholefield's neighbours were believed to be closely packed. So the Settlement Council was driven a step further on the path of self-annihilation. If the Education Committee would not accept the site of the Round Chapel for a nursery school, would the Parks Committee buy the whole Every Street property for an open space, leaving the North Wing of Ancoats Hall as a habitation for Miss Rogers and a centre for Settlement activities ? No, the Parks Committee was not prepared to pay a penny for it. Alternatively, would they recommend the City Council to take it as a gift ? Yes, they would. Accordingly, on May 25th, 1925, the Settlement Council minutes record the following resolution proposed by Professor Stocks and carried unanimously :—

That the Council accept the generous proposal of the Parks Committee to transfer the properties to the City Council forthwith. Resolved : that Sir Henry Miers, Mr. Ackroyd, Mr. Allen, the Warden and Hon. Secretary be and are hereby constituted a sub-committee to carry out the transfer to the City Council if the Parks Committee's proposal be accepted, and to make such arrangements as to the vacation of the premises, disposal of the material . . . and any other arrangements for the carrying on of the work as they may think necessary. Resolved : that if the Parks Committee's proposal be accepted by the City Council, the Trustees of the Settlement be directed to transfer those properties to the City Council, and that the Secretary be, and is hereby authorized to hand over the title deeds to the Corporation Authorities when they are required.

This resolution was moved by Professor J. L. Stocks. And as this is the first appearance of his name in the present record, so it was also his first appearance as a member of the Council. He had, in fact, been invited to join it soon

after his arrival in Manchester as successor to Professor
Samuel Alexander in the Chair of Philosophy.   An ex-Poor
Law Guardian, a former worker at the Rugby Boys' Club,
an active member of the W.E.A. and a friend of its founders,
it was considered suitable that he should have a hand in
any social service venture connected with his new University
—even though this should involve him in acting as its pall-
bearer.   To Miss Rogers, who had followed the proceedings
of the Council with growing disquiet and an agony of
apprehension for the future of her poverty-stricken neighbours, the advent of J. L. Stocks brought new hope.   Here
perhaps was someone, unwearied by the discouraging struggle
of the post-war years in Ancoats, who would understand
what the Settlement meant to its inhabitants.   Here was
someone to whom she could frankly express her profound
horror of the grievous capitulation about to be made by her
Council.   Standing amid the chaos of her office, she told
J. L. Stocks what she thought about it all.   To whom could
she appeal ?   She had her own answer to that question :
to the Trustees, without whose consent Settlement property
could not be disposed of.   And among the Trustees was·
Alice Crompton—the Warden of the golden age—now
separated from the Settlement by many years of work far
from Ancoats and by the physical affliction of almost
impenetrable deafness.   But the memory of Alice Crompton
was evergreen among the remaining Settlement Associates
and Miss Rogers had not lived for eight hard years in Ancoats
without realizing its significance.   Very well, then, Alice
Crompton should know what was afoot !

When Miss Rogers said " I shall write to Alice Crompton ",
J. L. Stocks gathered from her voice that a momentous
resolve had been declared, but not knowing Alice Crompton
he could not fully gauge its import.   Looking back upon the
incident in the light of later experience it seemed to him as
though he had stood in the presence of Aladdin at the precise
moment when Aladdin rubbed his lamp.

CHAPTER VII

RECONSTRUCTION

WHEN Aladdin rubbed his lamp, it will be remembered, a genie appeared. When Miss Rogers, acting desperately on her own responsibility, wrote to Alice Crompton, much the same result ensued. Alice Crompton appeared forthwith in Manchester. She did not, of course, arrive quite suddenly from nowhere in a clap of thunder and a sheet of flame, but she gave the impression of having done so. Nor was Miss Rogers's the only protesting voice which reached her. In fact, she arrived prosaically by train from Sussex, having talked the situation over with J. J. Mallon, and established herself in the house of her sister, a Manchester resident, from whence she set to work to organize the salvation of the Settlement. At her coming, memories of the golden age leapt in the minds of those who had known it—among the senior members of the University staff and the older Associates in Ancoats. Friends who had helped the Settlement in the past reawakened to the idea that it was still worth helping. A keen wind blew across the dusty scene. The atmosphere became exciting.

It was not, however, to any veteran of the golden age that Alice Crompton finally turned in her search for a principal executant of reconstruction, but to the newcomer, J. L. Stocks, whose first act as a member of the Settlement Council had been to move, with dour lack of enthusiasm, the resolution foreshadowing its dissolution. There were various reasons for this, but among them was the fact that J. L. Stocks had fallen in love at first sight with the Settlement's premises. For many months after his arrival he had prowled round the centre and purlieus of Manchester, learning its shape, absorbing its personality and unearthing its history. Wherever a building bore a date, that date was recorded in a small notebook. The cult of Manchester became increasingly absorbing; and when it led him, at the invitation of

Miss Rogers, to *Christchurch 1821*, his affections straightway settled there.

Yet to a newcomer the Every Street scene might have seemed discouraging if not downright repellent. The Settlement offices, entered by a separate door in the North Wing of Ancoats Hall and approached through a disused kitchen, were a wilderness of disorder. From their back windows one looked across a grimy slope—once the terraced garden of the manorial Mosleys—to the mean roof tops of Beswick on the farther side of the Medlock. Amongst them rose a forest of intermittently smoking factory chimneys. A little way down Every Street, the shapeless mass of the Recreation Room, known locally—and most appropriately—as the " Rec ", was the first piece of Settlement property to strike the eye. Between it and *Christchurch 1821* the tombstones which paved the intervening yard had become untidily uneven. But the curve of *Christchurch 1821* and the little square house which fronted it on Every Street exuded a personality which was immediately arresting. Inside the house Miss Rogers's domestic economy held sway. Enough said. Inside *Christchurch 1821* all the unseemly litter of the last defaulting tenant, the peeling of the plaster, the patches and puddles of intruding Manchester weather, the incongruous notice over an inner door which invited visitors to " Serve the Lord with Gladness "—all this dishevelment, plus a sour smell, was insufficient to obscure something that was held within the rotundity of *Christchurch 1821*. What was it ? The harmony of good architectural proportion ? The haunting fervour of forgotten men who in a dim past had served the Lord with faith if not with gladness ? Or some enduring vibration from the passions of hungry Chartists gathered in that place to voice a wrong and grasp a hope ?

There followed for the Settlement a period of inspiriting activity. The precise chronological sequence of its events is difficult to recapture since written records are scanty and three of the prime movers, J. L. Stocks, Miss Rogers, and Miss Cashmore, are not alive to tell the tale. Certain incidents, however, survive in memory. One is the first significant meeting between Alice Crompton and J. L. Stocks. Miss Crompton's deafness, in some respects an impediment, had one advantage. It enabled her to say what she wished without interruption and, by retaining full control of her amplifying instrument, to exercise a kind of chairmanship over the resulting discussion. On the occasion of this first interview she expounded at length her plan of reconstruction, embodying a public appeal and an indication of the persons and interests to be drawn into its orbit. This done, she handed the mouthpiece of her amplifier to Professor Stocks with a flashing smile, embodying the surrender of the eternal feminine to the leadership of the eternal masculine, and the words : " Now please, you must tell me exactly what you want me to do." He was, of course, by that time fully charged. It was the first personal impact upon him of Miss Crompton, and her plan was a positive one. Grasping the mouth of her amplifier he transmitted to her, with the authority of his professorial wisdom, all its main points.

A second incident concerns the resignation of Miss Rogers. The coming of Alice Crompton and all that followed from it brought to Miss Rogers a sudden relaxation of tension. Strong hands were stretched out to her Settlement ; she was no longer the only person who passionately cared ; its survival was, if not assured, at least probable ; a shining future of expanding usefulness and new pioneer work might lie ahead of it—given the right Warden. But was she the right Warden ? Many friends of the Settlement had doubts. Miss Rogers herself had none. She knew that she was not. " I am not the woman for it," was her brief and final verdict. Accordingly, she placed her resignation in the hands of the Council and the search for the right person began. It lasted from September 1925 to April 1926, and was brought to a triumphant finish by the appointment of Miss Hilda Cashmore.

The appointment of Miss Cashmore was not merely a triumph for the Settlement, it was an unexpected triumph. At the outset of the search no one would have dreamed of suggesting to Miss Cashmore that she should leave the Bristol

Settlement which she had built up and perfected by years of creative personal effort, in order to shoulder a gruelling and uncertain task of reconstruction in Ancoats. Moreover, Miss Cashmore was not only a Southerner born and bred, she was an incurable country lover. That she would be prepared to live for any length of time away from the flowers and trees and country smells of Mendip, and so very far away, would not naturally have occurred to anyone who knew her. Nor did it occur to J. J. Mallon, who at an early stage had been drawn into the reconstructive effort, when he invited her to cast her mind round the personnel of the social services for possible candidates. She knew, and was known to all the world of Settlements. She was the natural person to consult on such a matter. There was, however, considerable joy in Manchester when J. J. Mallon reported that Miss Cashmore had given him to understand that under certain conditions she might be prepared to undertake the job herself. Its difficulties challenged her creative genius. Its bleakness stirred her pity. Its possibilities, in its strange black cobble-stoned environment, roused her interest. In Bristol the Settlement was a going concern, and others well versed in the Cashmore tradition, were at hand to keep it so. In Manchester there was more to do. There was, in fact, an awful lot to do.

But if Miss Cashmore had not been conscious, when she took her first dubious look at Ancoats, that vital energy was stirring in its Settlement life, and that anyone who undertook its direction would be very vigorously sustained, it is probable that she would have speedily returned to Bristol. It is probable, too, that a factor in her decision to remain was the prospect of a working partnership with J. L. Stocks, with whose social outlook and habit of thought she instantly made contact. Her assimilation into the Stocks household occurred during her first tentative visit to Manchester. As a member of its family circle, during the next seven years she was to find encouragement, diversion and repose. And it is more than probable that she felt in the very air of Manchester, as she first breathed it, that freedom from convention, mental alertness and warmth of humanity which compensates newcomers for its physical atmospheric defects.

With the first faint prospect of Miss Cashmore's advent, Miss Rogers's heart leapt up. With its final achievement she sang in words of her own a *nunc dimittis*. Never did a servant depart more serenely in peace, or see more hopefully the promise of salvation. She knew that she was greatly loved in Ancoats by many whom she had indefatigably helped. But she was anxious not to distract attention from Miss Cashmore, in whom she had unbounded faith. Therefore, when the time came, she slipped out of the Wardenship very quietly and continued to serve Ancoats unobtrusively in other ways. She left Manchester in 1931, and the Settlement Report of that year records her departure. It " brought a great deal of work to the Settlement, as she had a large clientèle of poor people needing help of every kind. . . . We hardly knew till Miss Rogers left how much we depended on her."

Meanwhile, the work of reconstruction surged forward along various lines. One of the conditions which Miss Cashmore had indicated as necessary to her acceptance of the Wardenship had been that the Warden of the Settlement should function as director of practical training in connection with a projected Manchester University diploma in social studies. The realization of this condition, and the appointment of Professor Stocks to act as joint Hon. Secretary with Mr. Robertson in April 1926, tied the Settlement more firmly to its parent university.

But the most urgent problem was the repair and rearrangement of Settlement premises. The essence of a Settlement is a group of resident settlers. Since its divorce from the Art Museum which penned it in the north wing of Ancoats Hall, the Settlement had focussed no such group. Such rooms as it possessed had given temporary shelter to a gradually decreasing flock of migrants. Therefore another of Miss Cashmore's conditions was a structural alteration to the north wing which, by opening up the attic floor and making it fit for human habitation, would provide at least minimum accommodation and relative personal comfort for

a group of women residents. Men, since, she knew that
abundant life must include the stimulating clash and clinch
of male and female personalities with all its attendant risk of
entangled affections, could be housed at 20 Every Street.
The Recreation Room must be repaired as best it could—it
was hideous, but necessary as the only large hall available for
Settlement activities, and a little ingenuity could make it look
astonishingly gay within.   Inside 20 Every Street something
had to be done to make Miss Rogers's bedroom habitable by
less altruistic mortals ; its noises were not seemly and major
sanitary rearrangement was urgently required.   Outside it,
some better groundwork for the feet of little children than
the lugubrious tombstones of Dr. Scholefield's undertaking
must ultimately be provided.

So the work of re-building and repairing, painting, pointing, clearing and planting went forward. The Council,
recovering from its mood of black negation, first qualified,
then withdrew, its offer of free gift premises to the Corporation Parks Committee. With Alice Crompton and J. J.
Mallon flinging their demands far afield and acting as a
rallying point to all who had at any time loved and served
the Settlement, a public appeal was launched and promises
of financial support began to roll in—none too soon—for the
structural reconstruction already in hand was estimated to
cost £600 at the very least. But that was not all. The
Round Chapel had to be cleared and rebuilt or adequately
repaired. It could not, as it was, be longer endured. And
any such venture was likely to multiply the above quoted
estimate by ten. Moreover, to keep the expanded activities
which Miss Cashmore and the Council contemplated on the
boil, was going to need a proportionately expanded annual
income. Therefore the precise demand of the Settlement
was for a capital sum of £6,000 and an additional income of
£600. And this, in fact, was what the Council asked the
public to provide, at a public meeting held in the Town Hall
in the autumn of 1926. By which time Miss Cashmore was
established in Ancoats Hall surrounded by an ardent group
of settlers, backed by a re-invigorated and reinforced Council,
and working in day-to-day collaboration with Manchester

University, as personified by the philosopher-citizen, J. L. Stocks.

Under such conditions, and with Miss Marjory Lees appearing once again in Settlement history as a financial fairy godmother, the appeal went well. Miss Lees is one of those rare people who, having inherited wealth and leisure, chooses to expend both in the service of the locality responsible for their origin. As a result, Cheltenham, Bournemouth, Haslemere, and London, W.1, know her not. She is, however, known to a wide circle of northerners as " Miss Lees of Oldham ". But Oldham is not very far from Ancoats either in spirit or in mileage, and at every turn of the Settlement's long history Miss Lees has quietly stood by to help it.

But the appeal would not have gone well enough had not an event occurred, in the winter of 1926, which it would be invidious to describe as a " Godsend ", though from the Settlement's point of view it did indeed appear as such. An elderly, and in some respects rather eccentric lady, Miss Alice Bickham, a remote connection by marriage of Mr. T. C. Horsfall, died suddenly and alone in a small house at Altrincham, leaving the residue of her estate to the Settlement in which she knew him to have been interested. When priority commitments had been duly discharged it was found that this residue consisted of an astonishing accumulation of personal property. The bulk of it was stuffed into the small house at Altrincham where pictures hung two deep upon the walls. Some of it, however, had not been collected from the firms which had supplied it. Much of this property was of considerable value. Among the pictures were David Cox's *Haddon Hall* and Turner's *Falls of Terni*. Much of it was unsaleable at prices comparable with those which Miss Bickham had paid. Some of it was unsaleable at any price at all. Miss Bickham had indeed made some surprising purchases in readiness for the large house and garden which, it was believed, she some day hoped to establish. For how else could one account for her collection of new leaden garden labels such as ordinarily protrude from the flower-beds of public parks—or for the assemblage of wooden dairy implements ? For that matter, how else could one explain the whole accumulated medley of linen, furniture, china, silver, golf clubs, pictures—indeed, there seemed to be no end to Miss Bickham's purchases and no calculable bounds to their relevance.

For the Warden of the Settlement and the more active of her Committee members the problem was to get this property moved, classified, valued, and sold—apart from such things as linen and furniture of which the Settlement itself had need. There were times when its newly decorated Common Room looked like an antique dealer's warehouse ; times when the interest of its workers would switch suddenly from Ancoats to London, S.W.1, where the fortunes of Every Street seemed incongruously linked to the rise and fall of an auctioneer's hammer in Christie's sale room. It was a long job and at times an awkward one, this piecemeal disposal of the Bickham bequest, but in the end it produced considerably more than the £6,000 estimated by the Council as the capital cost of reconstruction—£9,000 odd, in fact ; enough and to spare !

As the job of liquidation went forward, so too another job went forward : the transformation of *Christchurch 1821* into *the Round House 1928*. Its roof was a dangerous liability. Its floor collapsed into its basement with the first shock of reconstruction. Only the round outer walls of the old structure were found to be serviceable for the new, but they held its personality and preserved its outward appearance. For the rest, all was new—from the steel frame roof to the water-tight basement equipped with club-rooms and baths ; from the kitchen and canteen opening into 20 Every Street at one end, to the wide shallow stage with its curved cyclorama at the other. It made a superb theatre, gracefully designed by the Manchester University Professor of Architecture—Professor Dickie. And outside its doors, smooth shale superseded Dr. Scholefield's tombstones, which were lined up, backs to the playground wall, to remain there as silent unobtrusive witnesses to its past without impediment to the feet of those who were about to mould its future.

Shortly after these happenings a stately old lady visited Every Street to see what was afoot there. Her name was Mrs. Bedford and she lived in quiet retirement at St.

Anne's-on-Sea. Meeting a Settlement member, she explained that as a grand-daughter of Dr. Scholefield, and one whose childhood was spent in No. 20, she had a natural interest in the place. She had, indeed, much to tell of life there in the doctor's time : of the arrangements of his house and chapel and of his sayings, handed down to the third generation. Among them was his deathbed charge to his daughters concerning the future of the chapel. " Use it for something, girls," he is reputed to have said. " You can use it for a circus if you like ; after all, it's round. It has served its time as a chapel." So it may be supposed that he would have approved the purpose, to which in its glorious resurrection from contempt and decay, it was about to be devoted.

On June 11th, 1928, the Round House was formally opened by Lord Crawford and Balcarres, Chancellor of the University of Manchester and newly-made President of its Settlement. Its opening was the occasion of the unveiling of a small shining link with the Settlement's past, which had been added to the structure of the Round House : a beautiful stained glass window commemorating the work of Eva Gore Booth in the Settlement's early days, and presented by her friend Esther Roper.

But the opening of the Round House was a mere formality. The curtain had already risen on the drama of a second golden age.

CHAPTER VIII

THE REIGN OF HILDA CASHMORE

IN the summer of 1926 Sir Henry Miers retired from the Vice-Chancellorship of Manchester University and from the Chairmanship of the Settlement which went with it. His last friendly gesture to the latter institution was a substantial contribution to its reconstruction fund. He was succeeded in both offices by Walter Moberly, now Sir Walter, whose first impression of the Settlement, as quoted in its Annual Report for 1926–7, is worth recording :—

" During my first year in Manchester I have gained two vivid impressions from my contact with the Settlement, both of which are confirmed and intensified by the Secretaries' Report. The first one is of the fresh and vigorous life which has been stimulated in all departments. New enterprises are being started, old enterprises are renewing their youth. Similarly, old friends of the Settlement are rallying to its support whilst it is rapidly making new ones both in Ancoats and in the University. I welcome particularly the keen interest which has been shown and the personal service which has been given by students of the University

" My other impression is that all this work is being carried on under a cruel handicap. There is far too little accommodation in the existing houses and there is little or no money in hand to provide more."

The Settlement was, in fact, though rich in capital, by no means assured of an annual income adequate to its wider ambitions. But it is with the first of Walter Moberly's impressions that we are for the moment concerned : the vigour and expansiveness of its new pulsating life, in the centre of which Miss Cashmore was cheerfully at work.

When Hilda Cashmore came to Manchester, the Council of the Settlement knew that they had acquired a Warden who, by wide repute in the social service world, would draw

residents and students to Ancoats. They knew that they
would find in her a pioneer of new works and a link with
settlement and social service movements of national scope.
But Hilda Cashmore was something more than an experienced and notable social worker. She was a very remarkable and positive personality. She inspired in her fellow-
workers great devotion, and on occasions great hostility.
There was in her an element of austere saintliness. She
would have followed her Saviour into the homes of the poor
and the infectious sick—into the wilderness and up the hill
of Calvary. But it is doubtful whether she could have
brought herself to follow Him into the dining-room of a
rich Pharisee, and in this she would perhaps have disappointed Him, as on occasions she disappointed the rich
and hospitable citizens of Manchester. Yet with this
austerity and a self-withdrawal which was on occasions
baffling, she mingled a humour so merry, an imagination
so vivid, and an æsthetic sense so penetrating, that contact with her was an adventure and an inspiration, and where
she lived and worked, there life flowed warm and strong
and in all its varied phases intensely interesting. She
was not at her best on committees, though her work constantly demanded her presence at them. She was at her best
in her personal contacts with human beings and their
problems and in the creative effort of devising new ways
of meeting them. She was a pioneer rather than an administrator. In this respect she found in J. L. Stocks the ideal
collaborator, since he was a perfect committee man and a
wise administrator.

With Hilda Cashmore, there arrived also from Bristol
Winifred Gill, who was to live and work with the Warden
as " free-place " resident. Miss Gill's precise function on
the Settlement staff would be difficult to define. She was
no kind of an administrator, held little traffic with the social
sciences and seldom appeared on a committee. Had she
done so, she might have declared in the words of Stella
Benson's ghost :—

> " I will enliven your austere committees
> With stories gleaned among the Seraphim ! "

She was, however, an artist in all she did, working in any material that came to hand. She could produce pictures, embroideries, stage sets, sweets and musical instruments. Weeds in a jam-pot became beautiful in her hands. The most humdrum environment yielded arresting and hilarious stories. From the surrounding junk-shops she extracted objects of rare interest. Children found her ways thrilling. Middle-aged women citizens followed her on sketching expeditions. She was an essential part of the new life generated in Ancoats, and a significant factor in its rich variety.

For the rest, where Miss Cashmore came, residents came : more in fact than the Settlement premises could hold. In the first year of her reign there was an overflow into lodgings. But some relief came at the beginning of the Session 1928–9 with the acquisition by a member of the Settlement Council of two small cottages in Every Street : one of them a corner shop, firmly occupied, the other, No. 21A, available for letting to the Settlement as a habitation for the Warden and Miss Gill. No. 21A was a typical Ancoats slum house, "two up and two down", and its first requirement was a drastic stripping of woodwork for the eviction of certain previous tenants with whom the Warden could not live in comfort. In other respects 21A Every Street was the habitation of her choice. Its occupancy brought her nearer to her street—nearer to her neighbours.

To the old Associates, the Settlement's revival brought sheer delight. Many of them looked back upon an earlier golden age. They had been the companions of Alice Crompton and of J. J. Mallon. Some of them, indeed, had greeted Alice Crompton's return with a request to the Council that she should once more become their Warden. They had kept the Field Club alive. They had kept the Warden's Tuesday "at homes" alive. Miss Cashmore found 20 of them holding the fort, and they received her with rapture. Two years later their membership had risen to 100, and the equipment of the new Round House was helped forward by a two days' bazaar organized by them. Mr. Gandy Bewick, Mr. Watson, Mr. Robinson, Mr.

Stewart, Mr. Farrell—these names and many others recur in the records of Settlement activity during this period. Some indeed had recurred since the beginning of its history. Mr. Gandy Bewick had been present at its inaugural meeting. The comradeship of the Settlement was once again a joy to them. " Here we rub shoulders with University Professors and more than rub shoulders with Miss Cashmore ", said one of them after an unusually stimulating social evening. The new Constitution of the Settlement, about which more will be said later, gave them two representatives on the Council, and they justified their representation by ardent, unrelaxing co-operation in Settlement affairs.

Another activity which showed unbroken continuity from early days—like the Associates and partly because of them—was the regular gathering of blind men and women for reading aloud and tea on Monday afternoons. The formerly disused kitchen in the North Wing of Ancoats Hall, which had become a " Parlour " under the reconstruction scheme, was the scene of this undeviating activity. With the help of friends in the West Country, from whence Miss Cashmore came, this Parlour was kept full of flowers and other objects reminiscent of country life and likely to interest the children of Ancoats. No doubt the Monday visitors enjoyed the smell, if not the sight of them.

But the real centre of life was in the reconstructed Round House. The Warden had a thirst for dramatic production and the Bickham bequest had provided her with a superb stage. From the streets of Ancoats and the lecture-rooms of the University actors and actresses rose up at her call. J. L. Stocks found a new and unexpected vocation. Drama had been an old settlement activity in Manchester. It is an almost universal settlement activity elsewhere, and not without good reason, since few activities transcend so imperiously the differences of age and sex and class. But with the acquisition of the Round House stage, drama came into its own in Ancoats. Its Nativity Plays were the great event of Christmas and two of them,[1] home-made,

---

[1] *Everyman of Every Street* and *King Herod*, by M. D. Stocks (Sidgwick & Jackson).

achieved with subsequent publication, a wider audience. It was a proud moment for the Settlement Players when the Dean of Manchester, witnessing a performance in the Round House, requested the transference of the entire production to the Cathedral, where with the backing of a superb choir and all the resources of Cathedral pageantry and vestment the Christmas drama was played out on an improvised stage under shadowy arches.

There were other proud moments provided by successive productions of *St. Joan*, *The Lady with the Lamp*, *Abraham Lincoln*, *Macbeth*. In Aileen Barr of the University Zoology Department, Ancoats found an inspired leading lady. Miss Gill's stage sets reached high peaks of excellence, and those who saw the curtain rise on the banks of the silver Loire or sunset over Bethlehem will not easily forget the gasp with which an Ancoats audience met a sudden onslaught of beauty. Nor will those who played *Macbeth* to a house packed with near neighbours from the Ancoats streets, forget the roar of excitment which, beginning as a murmur, rose to a crescendo with the oncoming " clop, clop " of Banquo's horse as he approached his waiting murderers. It is probable that most of those present had never met *Macbeth* as an exercise in classical English complete with glossary. They were thus able to receive it as a supreme blood and thunder melodrama. An added stimulus to this dramatic revival were the visits which from time to time the Arts League of Service made to the Round House in the course of its indefatigable missionary tours on behalf of music and drama. The Settlement Players watched with fascinated eyes not only the stage performances of these finished artists under the direction of Eleanor Elder, but their back-stage arrangements, the speed and skill of their fit-up and the perfect order and compactness of their properties. It was particularly interesting to trace the influence of these professional standards on the subsequent dramatic activities of the Junior Associates.

Like the Mediaeval Church, the Round House served many purposes. It was not only a theatre. Below ground level it was a honeycomb of clubrooms. From the beginning of 1929 onwards, during the middle of the day it was a luncheon club well patronized by school teachers, municipal officers, and other social workers in the Ancoats neighbourhood. Time and again it was the scene of lectures and conferences, dances and supper parties. And from the Treasurer's point of view it had its uses as a source of income from letting.

Outside Ancoats a new revival of old activity was soon in train. Miss Rogers's holiday school project continued, with the help of the Manchester Education Committee and the Board of Education, as an annual event. But since the loss of the old Hayfield cottage the Settlement had possessed no country residence. In the first year of Miss Cashmore's reign a joint summer camp at Coniston brought Ancoats and Bristol citizens together under leadership familiar to both. At Easter 1927 an enterprising group visited Paris. Later a Settlement party of 11 got as far as Geneva. But in 1928 more permanent schemes for escape were set on foot. The Warden and J. L. Stocks began scouring the neighbouring hills and dales of Derbyshire for a purchaseable or leaseable camping site. To Southerners these regions are apt to present a somewhat unfriendly appearance. " Cold comfort farms ", blackened by the driven smoke of industrial Lancashire, cling to bare hillsides on which a landscape of windswept heather and bilberry combines the spacious loneliness of a Scottish moor with the inescapable grime of a London park. But these regions are dear to the heart of Lancashire, and there are few more inspiriting sights than that of a Manchester railway terminus early on a Sunday morning, thronged with the adolescent population of a great urban area, bound for the open spaces, equipped with rucksacks, shirts and shorts. For the farmers whose gates they often fail to close, the inhabitants of the villages round whose stations they crowd hilariously at sundown, and the clergy who consider that they ought to be at Church, there are perhaps certain lingering regrets.

On one such hillside, after much searching and an abortive negotiation elsewhere, the Settlement secured three acres of wind-swept earth's surface, within easy distance of Marple

Bridge Station. There, by the generosity of Mr. and Mrs. J. J. Todd, a snug and commodious camping hut was erected in memory of their son Douglas Todd, a medical student of Manchester University, cut off by sudden illness on the eve of his career. Let us suppose that the hut which bears his name has brought health and cheer to the boys and girls, mothers and babies, who might otherwise have been his patients, and that Douglas Todd has thus fulfilled his task of healing after all. At any rate, the Settlement camping ground at Ludworth was opened on May 3rd, 1930, since when innumerable dwellers in the heart of Ancoats have walked, camped, dug, rested, cooked, picnicked, drowsed and played in and round about the Douglas Hut.

Meanwhile there remained one more piece of internal reconstruction to be accomplished. New wine needs new bottles. The Settlement's constitution required overhauling, and with the acquisition of an increasing amount of property together with new responsibility, as will presently be shown, for property administered by others, there was a case for incorporation under the Companies Act. A Drafting Committee was appointed by the Council in November, 1926, and incorporation duly authorized in October, 1927. It was an expensive business and cost the Settlement £83 before it was completed. Indeed its final completion was only achieved in 1935 with conveyance to the Settlement of property still held in the names of the surviving Trustees. But with its new corporate constitution the Settlement acquired not merely a legal personality and a portentous seal, but an expanded and more widely representative Council and two new honorary offices : a Presidency, which was filled by Lord Crawford and Balcarres, in time for the opening of the Round House, and a Vice-Chairmanship to relieve the Vice-Chancellor of some of the routine duties involved by the Chairmanship. To this last office Professor Weiss, Professor of Botany in the University of Manchester and a proved friend of the Settlement since its early days, was elected as soon as it came into existence. He had in fact done the real work of it for some time. When he left Manchester in the Summer of

1930, J. L. Stocks succeeded to the job, which was in effect that of Chairman of the Executive. He was himself succeeded, as Joint Hon. Secretary, by Roger Wilson, the son of an old friend of the Settlement.

We must now follow Settlement activities into wider spheres. It was no new thing for the Manchester University Settlement to integrate its activities with movements of social ideas. Indeed the whole life of a Settlement, or a great part of it, is a reflection of such movements, and T. R. Marr in the far off days of his joint-Wardenship used his intimate knowledge of one part of the Manchester map as a starting-point for his concern with the whole of it. Miss Rogers, too, had been an indefatigable cultivator of social studies. But with the first throes of structural reconstruction past, Miss Cashmore carried this particular phase of Settlement activity a step farther; and as one of the principal architects of the British Association of Residential Settlements formed in 1920 she was well qualified to keep the work of her own settlement in step with what was being done by others. In Ancoats, her starting-point was an annual conference of social workers concerned with the various social services, both statutory and voluntary, operating in the district. Meanwhile a social survey group had set to work on a general review of the social services and resources of the New Cross Ward, which area provided the most accurate administrative definition of the neighbourhood hitherto referred to as Ancoats. A reference to this activity in the Annual Report for 1926–7 modestly confesses that the resulting survey " is hardly likely to be valuable as a permanent contribution to social study ", but " is teaching much to the residents and helpers who are engaged on it ". It did however evoke, in the course of the next two or three years, a number of useful studies,[1] the last of which : an investigation of the pros and cons of working-

[1] *Social Studies of a Manchester City Ward.* No. 1, A Study of the Health of Ancoats ; No. 2, Housing Conditions in Ancoats ; No. 3, Housing Needs of Ancoats in Relation to the Greenwood Act. *Some Social Aspects of Pre-War Tenements and of Post-War Flats,* by Avice Trench. (Published by the Manchester and District Regional Survey Society.)

class flats by Miss Avice Trench, may be regarded as a
notable contribution to the housing problem in general.

Miss Avice Trench had pursued her study of housing
problems as far afield as Vienna, as well as in London, Liverpool and other English cities. Her sojourn in 1930 and
1931 as a resident at the Settlement engaged on full-time
housing activities, brought it and its workers into particularly intimate contact with the housing ferment of these
years which centred on the Greenwood Housing Act of
1930. Manchester was, after all, the home of that indefatigable housing expert and practical reformer : E. D. (now
Sir Ernest) Simon. And its Housing Committee had in
the decade before the first world war undertaken a notable
programme of reconditioning of which Ancoats itself bore
structural traces. In the years with which we are now
concerned, E. D. Simon was continuing, by word and pen,
both locally and nationally, the campaign for better housing. His wife, Shena Simon (now Lady Simon) had succeeded him on the Council, and their joint effort as col-
laborators with Alderman W. T. Jackson, had been a significant factor in the rise on the southern outskirts of Manchester, of the model garden satellite town of Wythenshawe.
The Manchester Corporation Housing Committee was very
much alive. Large slum clearances were pending. With
this preoccupation in the forefront of all social work, with
the most active committee members of the Settlement in
close personal touch with the Simons, with E. D. Simon's
expert collaborator, Miss Marion Fitzgerald, in and out of
Ancoats Hall, and with the intractable problem of overcrowding, decayed houses, and disproportionate rents ever
present among its neighbours, it is not surprising that the
Settlement itself should have weighed in on 'the housing
campaign, and that some of the best energies of its workers
should have been focussed on its complications. They have,
in fact, never since been diverted.

But housing activities did not end with investigation,
study and propaganda. There were practical matters to be
attended to in a district such as Ancoats. The inhabitants
of its decaying houses needed help in their continual struggle

with house property owners—or rather with close-fisted agents, since slum landlords are seldom personified—for minimum repairs. A complicated network of legislation had to be operated on behalf of those for whose protection it was designed, many of whom were singularly ignorant of its possibilities. To meet this local need an information bureau on housing problems was established at the Settlement in the Spring of 1930. On Monday evenings, the blind having departed from the Parlour, a housing expert as knowledgeable in that particular branch of legislation as a poor man's lawyer, was in session at the " baroo " : for such, phonetically spelled, was its local designation. Not all the questions posed to it evoked answers as uncomplicated as the simple negative returned to the question : " Is it really true that my rent will be decontrolled if I marry again ? " Many of the personal problems brought to the " baroo " were referable to the Poor Man's Lawyer. Many required action by Settlement helpers : visits to the Town Hall to mobilize its coercive powers against penurious slum landlords. And foremost among such helpers Canon Shimwell, Rector of Ancoats, moved from house to house like an avenging angel. " Let justice be done if the ceiling fall," might have been his motto. With shoulders squared, underlip pugnaciously protruding, and a shrewd knowledge of municipal procedure, he hunted down grievances and hunted up statutes, with zest generated by first-hand knowledge of how his flock lived—and why many of them, in fact, failed to do so.

There is, however, another and more positive side to this concentration of Settlement activity on the housing problem, so important in its bearing on the history of the Manchester University Settlement, and indeed of all Settlements, that it deserves a chapter to itself. It will suffice at this point to recall the fact that while the inner ring of Manchester slums was showing such signs of decay as to call for wholesale demolition rather than piecemeal reconstruction, vast building developments were occurring in its outer suburbs of whose social problems the workers in Ancoats were not oblivious.

1930–1 was a significant year in many respects, politically as well as socially. It was the year during which the " economic blizzard " which had never ceased blowing in the industrial North since the slump of the immediate post-war years, reached gale force. It blew Ramsay Macdonald's Labour Government to shreds, bankrupted the Unemployment Insurance Fund with a debt of £115 million, and produced in Great Britain the phenomenon of " structural unemployment " concentrated in " special areas " imposed on the top of generalized wide-spread economic depression. Manchester itself was not part of a " special area " but, since unemployment is a highly infectious social disease, and since its great traditional industry was " structurally " affected by world trends, the economic blizzard blew pretty strongly through its streets, and Ancoats felt the force of it.

Unemployment insurance with its changing devices for prolonging uncovenanted benefits, backed by a Public Assistance Committee whose scale of allowances did not materially differ from insurance benefits, and whose conditions of outdoor relief were mercifully tempered to the hard times, kept sheer starvation at bay. But nothing that a relieving authority, whether P.A.C. or later, U.A.B., could do, was likely to penetrate the black cloud of unhappiness occasioned by enforced idleness, or obviate its progressively evil influence on physical, mental, and spiritual vitality. Moreover, under such conditions the expensive habit of living upon credit and running into debt for the purchase of necessary renewals of clothing and household goods added intensified complications to life on the margin of destitution. Some tribute must certainly be paid to the commercial acumen of those who introduced greyhound racing to the British public at this particular period of history, but its entertainment value and the prosperity which it brought to its promoters was poor compensation for its contribution to the social and economic problems of an impoverished locality or for the wave of commercialized gambling enterprise which accompanied it ; since gambling, like unemployment, is an infectious disease and their bacilli are not unrelated. The hopes of social workers rose with the appointment of a Royal Commission on Betting and Lotteries in 1932 and fell again with the Government's refusal to accept two of its major unanimous recommendations. Readers who wish to recapture the atmosphere of these years can achieve this unpleasant experience by re-reading Walter Greenwood's novel *Love on the Dole*. Though it relates specifically to an area of Salford on the farther side of the Centre of Manchester from Ancoats, its locality covers a segment of the same inner ring of slums and the conditions of life which it describes are not dissimilar.

By the time the economic blizzard reached gale force in Ancoats, the Settlement was happily a going concern with all its forces mobilized. The first reference to renewed depression occurs in the Annual Report for 1929-30.

" I cannot close this report," writes the Warden, " without reference to the hard times through which we are living. The burden of Unemployment and its retinue of ills, both spiritual and physical, make our work ever more necessary and more anxious. We do not wish to give relief. We think that to trifle with inadequate schemes of this sort would spoil our relations with a courageous and independent people and would do no good. . . . There are special dangers in a time of deep depression. One of the greatest is a recklessness fed by every hoarding and almost every newspaper, offering something for nothing. There is a sinister connection between no work and great inducements to gambling that sickens one's heart as one watches. As drinking decreases, gambling with all its evils seems to take firmer hold. . . ."

The Settlement's immediate work lay ahead clear. It must keep the lights burning brightly in the Round House and make, with ever increasing insistence, demands upon the creative instincts and mental calibre of its neighbours. Such a policy may be described as " escapism ". To which it may be replied that if an uncontrolled economic system closes the natural exit from apathy and discouragement the least the prisoner can do is to effect escape by another.

And the least the would-be liberator can do is to assist his flight—provided always that the make-shift exit is not mistaken for the main door, and held to be an adequate substitute for it.

In the early Spring of 1931, therefore, the Executive Committee decided to appeal to the Pilgrim Trust for money wherewith to occupy and train unemployed adolescents, both boys and girls, and premises in the reconstructed basement of the Round House were allocated for this purpose. The Pilgrim Trust responded generously, a special Pilgrim Trust account was opened, and two salaried leaders appointed for boys and girls respectively. But in the case of the girls, the Settlement had made a miscalculation. Girls, like women, are never unemployed in the sense of having nothing to do. If the labour market ceases to want them their homes become the more insistent. Their wages may stop, their work, never. At an early stage, therefore, the sum allocated from the Pilgrim Trust account for a girls' club was transferred to a club for unemployed men, and the Settlement became an " unemployed occupational centre " with an average daily attendance of 70— one of many springing up in the Manchester area and indeed all over industrial Britain.

One other short sharp activity arose from the unemployment situation. In the Spring of 1931 the Settlement was invited to play its part in an enquiry, for the benefit of the Royal Commission on Unemployment Insurance then in session, into the fate of unemployed persons disallowed benefit under the Unemployment Insurance Act of 1930. How were they living ? On landladies, on credit, on the P.A.C. ? The job involved a lot of visiting, widespread over the Manchester area, and subsequently, a good deal of classification. Those who took part in it learned a great deal about working-class lives in the trough of the great depression. Its value to the Royal Commissioners there is no means of assessing.

So much for the work of the reconstructed Settlement —or at any rate enough of it to account for an incoming Vice-Chancellor's first impression of new enterprise starting and old enterprise renewing its youth. What of his second impression : financial insecurity : the insecurity of heavy capital expenditure unsupported by an assured income ? In fact, this stringency dogged the Settlement and cramped its style throughout the whole period at present under review. In 1928 it had been hoped to build up an endowment fund from the residue of the Bickham bequest, but first a deficit in the year's working had to be extinguished by a transfer from accumulated capital. The following year produced a new deficit and the situation was redressed in 1930 by the deplorable expedient of depriving the Warden of a salaried housekeeper. Thereafter the economic blizzard was reflected in a smaller subscription list, reduced letting of the Round House, and larger claims on the Settlement's help. In 1931 subscriptions were down by £209, expenses up by £348. In the following year a contribution from the Pilgrim Trust account for rent and administrative costs helped matters, but 1932 produced a deficit of £213. Once again the Settlement was living on capital.

Nevertheless, fit was a going concern : humming with activity, thronged by its neighbours, revered by its city, closely linked to its University : a strong and venerable Settlement in the wider world of Settlements where Wardens met annually in conclave under the auspices of the British Association of Residential Settlements. Above all, it was an *interesting* Settlement. Looking upon this handiwork, so much of it her own, Miss Cashmore felt that she had done the job which she set out to do and that others awaited her. The first loosening of her bonds came as early as the Autumn of 1930, when she persuaded the Council to allow her to divide the Wardenship with Lady Mabel Smith. Lady Mabel Smith was well known to the world of education and Labour in the West Riding of Yorkshire. A keen politician and an active member of her County Education Committee, she represented an inspiriting left wing deviation from the Fitzwilliam dynasty from which she sprang. Ever ready to move swiftly and live strenuously, she was prepared to make a half-time job of the Ancoats Wardenship, relegating to the other half of her time the West Riding

County Council, the management of a large country house on the East side of the Pennines, and later, membership of the National Labour Party Executive. The inhabitants of Ancoats received her with delight as one of themselves. Contact with her involved no ice-breaking.

With Lady Mabel Smith thus semi-attached, it was possible for Miss Cashmore in the Spring of 1932 to slip out for a three months' visit of investigation into Indian conditions with which the Society of Friends, of which she was a member by convincement, were concerned. For Ancoats that visit was the beginning of the end. Deep as was its poverty, the poverty of India was infinitely deeper. The wide ocean of India's need made the need of Ancoats look small. Moreover, by this time Hilda Cashmore had done what she intended to do in Ancoats : she had made its Settlement a going concern. She had hoped to get the job done in three years. In the end it took seven. On the other hand, Manchester had proved less dour than she had at first supposed. In one respect only had it fallen short of new hopes and old traditions. Educationally, in the matter of continuous classes and literary studies, Ancoats would not come awake. Perhaps competing entertainments damped the thirst and blunted the human capacity for mental concentration. At any rate, it was not for want of trying. The second golden age could have provided its P. J. Hartog, its R. C. K. Ensor, its Miss Creak, and with the grant-aided machinery of the W.E.A. to back them up. For the rest, the vital human circle of residents and neighbours, helpers and visitors had revolved round Hilda Cashmore as a generation earlier it had revolved round Alice Crompton. There had been moments of triumph and exhilaration, of anxiety and discouragement, satisfying friendships, clashes of personality, much merriment, plays, supper parties, arguments, excursions—all the ingredients of family life lived to the full, for such, indeed, it is the business of a Settlement to provide.

The resignation of Miss Cashmore, Miss Gill, and Lady Mabel Smith was reported to the Settlement Council on February 22nd, 1933, and the quest for a new Warden began. In the following year Miss Cashmore set sail for

India to initiate under conditions even more remote from those of her beloved Mendip Hills, a settlement venture as exacting, as inspiring and as constructive, as that which had drawn her in 1926 to the unfamiliar chill and humid greyness of Ancoats.

THE ROUND HOUSE.
From a woodcut by Margaret Pilkington.

CHAPTER IX

COLONIZATION ON THE NEW ESTATES

THE more positive side of Settlement housing policy mentioned on page 79 and relegated because of its supreme importance to a chapter of its own, concerns the new municipal housing estates which were springing up on the outskirts of every town during the years which followed the first world war. The work of the Manchester University Settlement in connection with the Manchester Corporation estates was part and parcel of a widespread movement of social service which characterized these post-war years, and its activities were closely bound up with those of the National Council of Social Service whose New Estates Community Committee, operating from the Council's office in Bedford Square, London, promoted and co-ordinated such activities all over the country. But Manchester, true to its ancient boast, was well in the van of this movement and Miss Cashmore and J. L. Stocks may justly be named among its pioneers.

When J. L. Stocks arrived in Manchester in 1924, he went to live in Wilbraham Road, an " unadopted " thoroughfare running westwards into open fields from the main road out of Manchester to the South where it passes through the one-time village of Fallowfield. Manchester had in earlier years expanded starfish-wise along its main exits, the intervening spaces remaining unbuilt, except for old established country cottages and farms. Into such an area, Wilbraham Road, furnished at its Fallowfield end by a few large Victorian yellow-brick houses standing in their own grounds, led. On Sunday mornings University professors and *Manchester Guardian* leader-writers would use it as their starting-point for country walks. Its road surface was primitively rural, and on exceptionally clear days it offered long views to the South. At such rare times its inhabitants could even lift up their eyes unto the hills of

Derbyshire and Cheshire. But with the operation of the post-war Addison Housing Act in full swing, these amenities soon gave place to others. Wilbraham Road was " adopted " ; Corporation trams began to run on smooth concrete ; the dirty little Platt Brook which crossed it was incarcerated in a tidy sewer ; the handsome chain of red-brick wartime pigstyes which bordered it to the south were devoted to other uses ; trees were felled with a ruthlessness which later town-planners were to deplore ; and on the fields through which Wilbraham Road ran a large new Corporation housing estate of semi-detached cottages arose. In due course it was furnished with a church, a chapel, a school encircled by a spacious playground, also a branch public library which in the attractiveness of its structure, the intelligence of its staff, and the rich variety of its contents, far surpassed those institutions provided by private enterprise for the ratepayers of less favoured areas who are prepared to pay guineas a year for the privilege of not being dependent upon the social services.

The Wilbraham estate, for thus it was in due course named, was one of the earliest of the Manchester Corporation Estates, one of the largest, and one of the most prosperous. Its inhabitants represented various occupations and were drawn from various localities. There was as yet no wholesale removal of entire slum-cleared populations from the inner to the outer ring. This lent variety to the social scene, but on the other hand it meant greater personal isolation for its individual inhabitants. A neighbouring branch store of the Manchester and Salford Co-operative Society, with its dance-hall and its Women's Co-operative Guild, provided the beginning of social cohesion. So did the Church—for those who sought its ministrations. But where all were newcomers together, and newcomers from widely separated areas, there were no social roots, no common memories, no entangled family relationships, no time-honoured personal contacts with shops at which one's family had dealt for years. Something was missing from life which was not missing in the huddled mining communities of South Wales or the grimy streets of Ancoats. Was it possible

to fill this social hiatus by deliberately planting that which
in all existing human communities had struck its own roots
and expanded slowly as a native growth ? And if planted
deliberately, and of course carefully watered, would the
thing grow—or would the root fail to strike and its flower
wither as bedded-out flowers wither in a public park when
their season is past ?

To Hilda Cashmore, her mind drilling adventurously
into the future, it seemed as though the real need of Settlement activity might lie here rather than in Ancoats. Some
day the familiar shape of Ancoats would disappear in a town-
planning scheme for central Manchester, its rat-ridden
residential pockets neatly disentangled from its overshadowing warehouses and dusty yards, its streets widened, its
inhabitants thinned out. Meanwhile here on the Wilbraham Estate, and other estates, square miles of them all
over the place, all rapidly expanding and all much the same,
transplanted human beings were not as happy as gardens and
bathrooms and fresh air and elbow-room might be supposed
to make them. From these thoughts arose the resolve that
the Settlement must colonize. In other words, it must
embark on a venture of community building in the new
world.

To whom this thought came first, it is difficult to say. It
was germinating among the leading spirits of the newly-
formed National Council of Social Service in London ;
indeed there was much talk of it everywhere. But Hilda
Cashmore determined to act quickly in her own area. And
since J. L. Stocks inhabited one of the yellow-brick Victorian houses whose surburban dignity had been insulted
by the Wilbraham Estate and the trams which led to it, and
since he had nevertheless watched its growth with the
enthralled delight of an objective social-reformer, it seemed
that here in Wilbraham Road was an obvious field for the
great experiment. Accordingly we read in the Settlement
Council minutes of June 7th, 1928, that authority be given
to the Executive to proceed with a scheme for renting and
equipping a house on the Wilbraham Estate : No. 34 Tarporley Avenue, at a rent of 23s. 11d. a week, to be occupied

by Settlement residents engaged in social activities among
their estate dwelling neighbours. Thus the nucleus of a
New Estates Community Centre, which later became the
Wilbraham Association, was formed. Its formation of
course required and received the beneficent co-operation
of the Municipal Authorities, from whom the allocation of
a subsidized house during an acute housing shortage represented a considerable gesture of faith in the Settlement's
capacity to make good use of it.

Very many such Community Centres have since arisen,
and their history must be sought in the archives of the
National Council of Social Service by whom they have been
fostered and promoted, under whose auspices their experiences have been pooled, their finances supported, their
problems threshed out. When their collective history
comes to be written it will doubtless be seen that they dis-
play wide varieties of organization and control, and that
these variations have their origin sometimes in the character
of the estate itself; sometimes in the social ideals of the
community makers and the precise steps taken by them to
initiate community activities; sometimes in the local
authority's attitude to voluntary organization. On some
municipal estates community centres have been supplied
by the local authority as one among other social services
bestowed and administered from above. In others beneficent voluntary organizations have supplied the premises
and administered the services connected with them. Others
again, show a larger element of spontaneous co-operation
and active self-government. An estate inhabited largely
or even exclusively by the very poorest tenants forcibly
evicted from demolished slum property is clearly less capable of spontaneous co-operation or continuous self-government than one inhabited by tenants who, on their own
initiative, have sought improved accommodation, and who
have already practised the art of community living in
Co-operative Guilds, trade unions, chapels and political
parties. By such tenants, in these early days of large-scale
municipal building, was the Wilbraham Estate tenanted.
And the initiators of its community organization held before

themselves and their neighbours on the Estate, the ultimate ideal of complete and unassisted self-government.

This involved the slow encouragement of, at first, unrelated activities by groups of neighbours. Since gardening appeared to be the most enthralling activity of the men, and is incidentally one which offers shining opportunities for collective action in the acquisition of expensive tools and the joint large-scale purchase of materials, a Garden Guild was brought into being. At the same time a Wilbraham branch of the Manchester Women Citizens' Association was formed. But the cuckoo-like practice of pursuing such activities in the nests of other organizations was clearly a limiting factor. A community association can scarcely exist without a roof over its head and a dance-floor under its feet. The first major community activity therefore to focus the energies of the various separate groups was the building of a hall, and here the Settlement as an authoritative body capable of negotiating with the Corporation of Manchester, had to take the initiative. Governed by a limited number of houses to the acre, the planning of the Wilbraham Estate had produced some oddly-shaped residual open spaces. One of these, a strip running North from Wilbraham Road to its tributary Hart Road, offered possibilities as the site of a Community Hall. Once again the Municipal Authorities were responsive and on November 6th, 1929, the Settlement's magnificent new seal set its stamp on a lease from the Corporation to the Settlement, of the Hart Road site.

In October, 1930, the Wilbraham Hall was opened. Its building, the collection of funds on its behalf, the clearing of its surrounding land, the local organization required to guarantee its proper maintenance and the liquidation of the debt with which it opened its existence, all these responsibilities and the multitudinous negotiations which they entailed, demanded enthusiasm and initiative from the tenants. They were wisely led by their near neighbour J. L. Stocks and later by Miss Emily Jenkinson who, in response to a call for help, had returned to the Settlement as a resident, with a special mission to the Wilbraham Estate. She undertook the secretaryship of the newly-formed cómmittee representing the affiliated bodies already at work. J. L. Stocks became its Chairman, 34 Tarporley Avenue its administrative centre, J. L. Stocks's study its committee room. And " the people had a mind to work ". They wanted that Hall. They wanted to talk in it, to dance in it, to act in it, to let it to one another for wedding parties, to organize May festivals and fêtes in its grounds. And if a beneficent plutocrat had presented it to them ready equipped, faultless and debtless, it is very probable that they would not have wanted it quite so much.

So the Wilbraham Association grew and flourished, its model garden flowered, and leaders arose among its members. The Settlement had done much by its initiative to set the venture on its feet. The Carnegie Trust, through the medium of the N.C.S.S. New Estates Community Committee, did one thing more. It guaranteed a salary which enabled Miss Jenkinson to act for 5 years as full-time General Secretary to the Association. It was an active and constructive period. Miss Jenkinson was a person of very varied talents. On the social service side she was alive to the needs of her colony. When economic depression spread over the Estate and many of its members faced poverty as discouraging if not as sordid as that which fell upon Ancoats, she was ready with an unemployment occupational club and other forms of emergency help. But a community centre is in its essence a co-operative society rather than a social service agency, and it is in the promotion of cultural activities that her work during this period stands out most clearly. She wrote melancholy haunting plays of the Celtic twilight and produced them with great ingenuity in the Wilbraham Hall. Skilful actors emerged from among her neighbours and stimulated by her example they, too, began to write plays. Demand and supply are blades of the same scissors and it is difficult to say which does the cutting; but whether stimulated by the interest of the Wilbraham tenants or itself a stimulus to them, the Wilbraham branch library amassed upon its shelves the most complete and topical collection of published plays that any student of modern drama could wish to find; all of which helped.

But Miss Jenkinson's greatest achievement is the fact that when her stipulated time as General Secretary came to an end in December 1934, and a larger job called her to London, the Wilbraham Association was able to stand alone. It had not merely grown, it had grown up, and must at this point disappear, like the Invalid Children's Aid Association, from the history of its parent organization.

It is thus that one would wish to see the British Empire administered, and there is still time for the Government to appoint Miss Jenkinson as Governor of one of our Crown Colonies.

But the colonizing activities of the Settlement had only begun. With the Wilbraham experiment well and truly launched, there remained other virgin fields to plough. Early in 1931 Miss Cashmore's attention turned in the direction of Newton Heath, another Corporation estate, and one which was both geographically and socially nearer to Ancoats. Its people were poorer, its air smokier, and its occupational make-up more industrial and therefore more susceptible to the economic blizzard than was the case at Wilbraham. Its need for outside encouragement was therefore so much the greater. By the end of the summer of 1931 two Corporation houses, Nos. 5 and 7 Surbiton Avenue, had been allocated to the Settlement by the ever responsive Housing Committee. Miss Gill and a fellow resident moved into one; Mr. Roger Wilson, the Settlement's new Joint Hon. Secretary, who had recently acquired a wife as public spirited as himself, set up house in the other. The two households, whose occupants like their neighbours went out to work by day, provided a vital and gay nucleus for social life.

For about eighteen months they " felt their way "; finally, with the help of such fellow-tenants as they had managed to gather round them and interest in the project, a community centre scheme was launched and the Newton Heath Guild of Neighbours came into being. There were 950 houses on the Estate. 300 of them were soon contributing weekly sums to the building of a hall. It was not a very commodious hall ; it was indeed a second-hand hut some 60 feet by 20. But its removal from its original site, its dismantling and its re-erection, was enthusiastically undertaken by the voluntary labour of the tenants who wanted · it—and doubtless, as at Wilbraham, the cost and labour of getting it made them want it more.

Here, too, we must take leave of the Newton Heath Guild of Neighbours ; not, however, because its fate diverges from that of the Settlement, but because it belongs to a later chapter of Settlement history. Suffice to say here, that we have reached the point at which other community centres were in being in other parts of Manchester and under other auspices. Here, as elsewhere in Great Britain, housing authorities and social reformers had become " community centre minded." But the Manchester University Settlement did the pioneering, and its " godchild " the Wilbraham Association is sure of a place when the history of this significant movement of inter-war social service comes to be written, for it was, in fact, the first.

CHAPTER X

IN May, 1933, the Settlement appointed Mr. and Mrs. Wyatt as joint Wardens, and Mrs. Wyatt stepped into Miss Cashmore's shoes as director of practical training in connection with the University Social Science Diploma. It was a job which, as an experienced social worker and ex-Secretary of the Institute of Hospital Almoners, she was very well qualified to perform. But the conditions under which she had to perform it were unfavourable. The more active a Settlement, the more difficult it is to transform its Warden into the dual personality of administrator and tutor. The two are in perpetual conflict. The work of the Settlement has to be done and if a trainee can do it the Warden *qua* administrator is tempted to leave her to it for the work's sake ; while the Warden *qua* tutor feels impelled to move her on to something else for the training's sake. Miss Crompton was faced with no such inner conflict. Miss Cashmore was, and the Settlement's urgent needs got the upper hand. As a result her diploma trainees sometimes grumbled. The situation is not dissimilar to that which arises in a busy hospital at moments when the probationer nurse is conscious of feeling more like a ward maid than a student. It is probable that the two functions should never be concentrated on the same person : at any rate that was the conclusion finally reached both by Manchester University and Mrs. Wyatt when on her resignation in 1940 it decided to appoint a Director of Practical Studies other than the Warden of the University Settlement.

Mr. Wyatt came to the Settlement straight from schoolmastering. Long absorption in social problems and out-of-school activities had led him to it   Something of a boy himself, with a boy's passion for making things out of other things, he was gloriously at home among the Settlement clubs, and capable of really enjoying himself in the company

of their members. This is perhaps a more valuable qualification for work among the young than the most sustained
effort of the will to do them good. It is a natural gift,
which cannot, like the will to do good, be acquired by prayer
and fasting.

As far as the Settlement's work was concerned, the Wyatts
inherited a going concern. Miss Cashmore's reign had
produced a multitude of inspiring activities. And Miss
Sheila McKay, a former Warden's Secretary, had, as acting
Warden during a brief interregnum between Miss Cashmore's going and the coming of the Wyatts in September
1933, held things together. As to the Settlement's reputation and outside contacts, here too the Wyatts entered
upon a goodly heritage. It had many friends, especially
in University circles, and there was no fear of intellectual
isolation for the new Wardens. But they were very soon to
discover that the finances of their new kingdom were in a poor
state. The wolf was at the door—indeed he seemed to have
established himself as resident doorkeeper at the Settlement.
Thus the first Annual Report for which the new Wardens
are responsible, records in addition to an impressive record
of old activities and some interesting new ones, a treasurer's
report in which the following ugly facts are stated : " Our
overdraft at the bank is £1,120." " Our securities are
valued at £1,741." " The loss on last year's work was
£614." This makes it clear that if the Settlement were to
go on living on capital it was not likely to live very long.
In a foreword to the Report the Chairman of the Executive
makes the familiar appeal for £600 more annual revenue.
And once more the familiar words appear : " The continued
existence of the Settlement is at stake." From which it will
be seen that in some respects the Wyatts' inheritance was
not quite such a going concern as its multitudinous activities
and its reputation might suggest.

They were not, however, easily discouraged. The wolf
at the door received them with a snarl and continued to snap
at their heels, but their neighbours and fellow-workers
gave them a ready welcome. J. L. Stocks was a firm friend
and an energetic colleague, and one who was constantly on

the spot. When Sir Walter Moberly departed in 1935 from the Vice-Chancellorship of the University and the Chairmanship of the Settlement, Ancoats lost a good friend. But in Professor (now Sir John) Stopford, his successor in both offices, it gained another ; a tried and devoted Manchester man, with a true Mancunian concern for the affairs of his City outside the walls of the University, and an effortless capacity for making direct and easy contact with all kinds of people.

With this considerable turn-over of personnel, activities suffered no setback. Indeed in dramatic work they swelled to new heights of ambition with the advent in February, 1934, of Miss Frida Stewart, to remain for two years as resident producer. Miss Stewart was a very remarkable person. With a delicate and diffident charm of manner amounting at times to a gentle vagueness, she combined an insistence which drew talent into her Round House net from wide and unexpected circles. This capacity was helped by the fact that with a Cambridge family background she knew large numbers of gifted people all over the place. She could, when occasion called, mobilize her own family and a wide circle of friends to produce visiting musicians for Ancoats. With such support the imaginative scope of her productions was prodigious. They lacked the detailed finish which Miss Cashmore had achieved by intensified drilling of her cast. But their setting, their movement, their casting, showed a talent which at times amounted to genius. For years some of the keener spirits among the Settlement players had cherished a longing to see De La Mare's *Crossings* played upon a stage but had funked its difficulties. Frida Stewart looked them in the face and drove the production through them. She staged Purcell's *Fairy Queen* and persuaded the Manchester College of Music to provide the backbone of an orchestra. With equal zest she attacked left-wing impressionist drama of the ultra-modern school, undaunted by its need of slick movement and complicated spot-lighting. The intellectual demands which she made upon Ancoats were as exacting in a way— though in a different way—as those made in the distant past by Miss Creak and Sophocles. And in these exhilarating ventures the Wardens aided and abetted her with all the resources at their disposal. From the reader's point of view it is regrettable that Miss Stewart's subsequent adventures as a supporter of the Spanish Republicans, and later as a successful escaper from a German concentration camp, lie outside the scope of this chronicle. Departing from Ancoats in the Summer of 1936 after ringing down the curtain on an admirable production of *The Beggar's Opera*, she left a flourishing dramatic group and an inspiriting tradition to be carried on by succeeding producers.

The Wardens certainly backed Ancoats drama with all the resources at their disposal, and among such resources was the Pilgrim Club. A new financial problem which they were called upon to face had been the reduction of its Pilgrim Trust grant. This was partly met by the winding up of the boys' club—no great loss. It had never flourished. But the Men's Club had to be carried on, and the shouldering of its overhead charges meant a new drain on Settlement finances at a moment when their prospects appeared to be clearing a little as the result of renewed appeals, further economies, and a magnificent contribution of £400 from the students of Manchester University out of the proceeds of their Annual Rag.

The Pilgrim men's club had to continue because unemployment continued. The economic blizzard was slackening in the country at large. But such storms leave a lot of debris on the beach. As the tide of depression recedes, those whose vitality has been sapped by prolonged unemployment remain unemployed and often unemployable. And the years which are marked by recession from the great slump of the early thirties and end with the hectic armaments activity of the late thirties, are also those which cover the advent of the Unemployment Assistance Board with its dual task of relief and rehabilitation. It was perhaps inevitable that the first should take precedence. At any rate, there was small prospect of rehabilitation for the economic casualties of Ancoats during these middle years of the nineteen-thirties. The returning tide of economic activity was slow to reach them, and the transfer from P.A.C. to

U.A.B. produced personal problems which called for neighbourly help. The Manchester P.A.C. had dealt pretty
generously with its dependants and there was little enthusiasm among them for a change of paymaster. All of which
meant further calls upon Settlement help and guidance.
So the Pilgrim men's club had to go on.

It went on with redoubled zest, under the resourceful
leadership of Mr. Richard Heath. It produced carpenters,
painters, scene-shifters and players for Miss Stewart's productions, and she in turn produced skilled direction and encouragement for its own productions, sometimes the work
of its own playwrights. On occasions it produced crowds
for the Manchester Repertory Theatre at Rusholme. It
produced painters and decorators working enthusiastically,
under the direction of Mr. Price Nunn of the Manchester
School of Architecture, for the rejuvenation of the Round
House. It patched up the " Rec " which a contemporary
report describes as an " indispensable but repulsive black
ruin ". It rebuilt the play-ground wall. It organized a
canteen at which the families of its members, and indeed
all Ancoats, could buy dinners as cheap as voluntary cooks
and scullions and freedom from overhead charges could
make them—and even a little cheaper as Settlement accounts
show. It contributed an Ancoats contingent for the South-
East Lancashire and North-East Cheshire Advisory Council
for Informal Education and Voluntary Activity with the
Unemployed—popularly known as S.E.L.N.E.C. And
by these activities it generated in its own members a sense
of being wanted. Incidentally it produced a number of
visitors for the Wardens' country cottage at Edale. This
small, secluded residence, some 30 miles from Manchester's
centre, had been acquired by Mr. and Mrs. Wyatt in order,
to preserve, for the benefit of their schoolboy son, some
semblance of family life in healthy surroundings. And the
Wardens had visions of quiet week-ends. The annals of
the Pilgrim Club, and indeed of other bodies attached to
the Settlement, suggest, however, that it often functioned
rather as a holiday home for their neighbours than as a
place of repose for themselves.

Closely connected with the Pilgrim Club, because largely patronized by the wives of its members, was the shop, started by Mrs. Wyatt in March, 1934. It was open every week for the sale of second-hand clothes contributed by friends of the Settlement and where necessary patched, cleaned, and renovated by its active helpers. It was in the nature of a running jumble sale and many a good bargain was to be found in it. In the end it proved to be " twice blessed " since it brought good bargains to the Settlement's impecunious neighbours and a substantial trading revenue to the Settlement's precarious finances. Incidentally it brought new confidential neighbourly contacts between those who bought and those who sold.

So life in Ancoats went on, with the Settlement as its centre of light and leading. Rendel Wyatt was ever ready to " dig, hammer, chop and saw " with groups of varying age composition. Jean Wyatt, with long experience of the social services, was ever ready with advice and help. Their Morris car rattled itself into a decline over stone setts, driven by all and sundry in the service of Ancoats. Their country cottage rang with the cheerful activity of Ancoats neighbours. Their hospitality was inexhaustible and ingenious. Under the management of Mr. and Mrs. D. L. Elliott the Tuesday " at homes " continued at full blast their unbroken record of conviviality. The *Mustard* Club was formed to give Settlement workers new opportunities of meeting. A mysterious and ancient fraternity known as the *Bread and Butter Club*, associated with the name of J. J. Mallon, sprang into activity on a visit from him. Hot-pot suppers in the Round House, to honour distinguished visitors or wind up theatrical ventures, brought friends together from near and far : Pilgrim Club and University, Ancoats and Didsbury, past and present.

But four disruptive events were casting their shadows before : slum clearance ; the departure of J. L. Stocks ; insolvency ; and in the end, the " black-out."

No one, other than the owners of slum property and those who, knowing that one thing leads on to another, make common cause with them, could regret Manchester's determination to make vigorous use of the powers conferred on local Housing Authorities by the Greenwood Act. Browning's *Bishop Bloughram* says, " Once cut the Liquefaction, what remains but Fichte's clever cut at God Himself ? " Adapting this conception to politics there are those who say : " Once interfere with a man's right to receive rent from an unhealthy dwelling, and what remains but the nationalization of land, or the municipalization of milk distribution ? An attack upon one form of property right must be regarded as an attack upon all forms and as such be resisted." There was no one within the Settlement's orbit, however, who argued thus. There were of course Ancoats dwellers who clung like limpets to their rickety homes because they were homes and set in familiar surroundings. But not a social worker, not a committee member, could regret the approaching destruction of Ancoats, least of all the Wardens who knew its darker side and worked day by day among its human victims. Such regrets as there might be were irrational sentimental regrets and recognized as such. They were the kind of regrets that sometimes assault the consciousness of a soldier who survives a war and allows his memory to brood selectively on its comradeship, its triumphs and its relaxations. And as we have seen, the Settlement had already taken steps to secure its own future, similar to those by which human beings conscious of their individual mortality ensure physical survival. It had begotten offspring. The Wilbraham Association had grown up. The Newton Heath Guild of Neighbours was still in a state of tutelage, and the departure of Mr. and Mrs. Roger Wilson in February, 1935, from the Settlement, from Surbiton Road and from Manchester, deprived it of valuable support before it had learned to walk alone. But the Settlement still had its second colony. And in October, 1935, new opportunities for service in a rehousing area had been opened up, with the establishment of a Settlement worker, Miss Pollard, as a tenant of Kennet House : a huge new block of Corporation flats in the Smedley area to the north-east of Manchester. Here was a different range of human need to be explored. Miss Trench's survey of life in post-war flats had already given some indication of its urgency.

In April, 1936, the City Council declared the New Cross Ward to be a " clearance area ". The Annual Report of that year refers to this declaration and reminds its readers of the profound effect which it will have on the future of the Settlement. It records the appointment of two committees : a sub-committee of the Settlement Council to make suggestions as to the functions of the Settlement as and when the change in its surroundings takes place, and a joint committee of Settlement representatives and representatives of the Manchester Better Housing Council, whose purpose was to work in co-operation with the Municipal Authorities for the assistance of tenants in the clearance area. It was of course known that the process would be a long one ; a glance at the procedure laid down in. the Greenwood Act gives some idea of how long ; and it was realized that the pace of demolition must keep step with the pace of rehousing in other areas. But it was calculated that in the course of the following five years or so, some 2,000 families would be leaving Ancoats, and that some 400 would, if the Housing Committee's plans matured, be re-settled in flats in or near the Settlement.

Would the resettled flat-dwellers need the Settlement ? Would its already considerable circle of friends from outside the area continue to look to it, and if so, for what purposes ? Or did its destiny lie outside Ancoats altogether, in the new areas with their interminable concrete roads and avenues, their sameness, their strangeness, their rootlessness ? Or in the great rabbit-warrens of Corporation flats with their communal staircase problems, their unneighbourly congestion, their screaming gangs of children, and their unfinished symphonies of wireless music on hot nights when windows must be open and there can be no silence for the tired, the sick, or the contemplative ?

Here was a job then, not merely of immediate social service, but of social scientific thought : systematic enquiry, and planning. The Settlement had, as we have seen already, carried through a number of surveys, either for publication or for use by responsible bodies. In 1935 it was able to distil, from Pilgrim Club personal contacts, a reply to the request of the U.A.B. for information concerning clothing clubs and replenishment schemes. In the same year its Young People's Advisory Committee conducted a sample enquiry for the Manchester area into the hours of boy workers in unregulated trades, to be offered as evidence to the Departmental Committee on the subject then in session. In the following year, a small group of enquirers presented a critical report on the working of the local Juvenile Employment Bureaux, while another supplied a Departmental Committee with evidence concerning Holidays with Pay. But the rehousing of Ancoats presented a larger field for enquiry into two sets of conditions : those from which human beings came : those to which they went, and the effect of the change on individual families. Incidentally, on the result of such an enquiry and the needs revealed by it would depend the Settlement's future line of action.

Thus the Settlement's great rehousing survey was projected. And from 1936 onwards it becomes a major pre-occupation. The Carnegie United Kingdom Trust which had backed the Wilbraham Road venture was prepared to back this new venture to the tune of £500, provided the Settlement was able to raise the balance of £283, estimated as its total cost. Of this, promises amounting to £176 were immediately received ; out of its own narrow resources the Settlement guaranteed £70, and the work started. Mrs. Wyatt was appointed as its Secretary, and extra help was provided for the discharge of her ordinary duties as Joint Warden.

By the end of 1938 the first stage of it, the enquiry into the conditions of those about to be deported, was completed. Of 600 families visited, 476 had willingly co-operated in the enquiry ; many of them were, of course, old friends of the Settlement, confident of its desire to help them through the ordeal of deportation. For the rest, the method of sampling was resorted to. As Mrs. Wyatt points out in a statement published in the Annual Report for 1937,

the Survey could show no final results until its second
stage was reached, as its real objective was a comparison of
conditions, family by family, in old and new surroundings.
But this interim statement yields some interesting conclusions. It confirms the impression that Ancoats is not
merely a community, with much of the " village " feeling
about it, but that it is an established community of families
with long tenancies. In addition to this, and largely because of it, it is a related community. It is recorded that
of the households visited, 190, or 41·27 per cent. had occupied the same house for over 20 years ; that of the 185 who
had a less than five years tenancy, 117 were Ancoats families
born of Ancoats parents ; and that of 476 families, 259 had
relatives in the clearance area ; of which 259, 141 were recorded as being dependent on their relatives for some
essential service.

She concludes her brief interim statement with the reminder that much apprehension exists among those whose
homes are scheduled for destruction and points out that
this is intensified by the long-drawn period of tension involved by Housing Act procedure. Two and a half years
after the scheduling of the area for clearance, the actual
date of demolition was still uncertain. As a result, repairs
remained undone, house-pride wilted, overcrowding waited
for official " clearance ". " The coming year should, however, show a definite move towards clearance and rehousing.
Some twelve months after the first of the families are re-
housed we shall visit again, and the second stage of the
Survey will have begun." These words were written in
the Autumn of 1938. By the Autumn of 1939 events both
in the world at large and at home in Ancoats had relegated
that " second stage " to an uncertain future.

But the business of demolition and rehousing was by
that time under weigh. The end of 1938 saw its beginning.
First the exodus of human beings and their movable property.
Then fumigation. Then, for a while, rows of silent, blind
and blackened houses. Then demolition. Like the fateful
hacking of Tchekov's *Cherry Orchard*, the pick and shovel
sounds in Ancoats. Lonely and majestic the Settlement

Buildings, flanked by the Public Library, stand out in their scarred landscape.   To-day

    " Cockle, spurge, according to their law
      Might propagate their kind with none to awe."

Vegetation is once more growing in Every Street, and an inhabitant directing a stranger has been heard to say : " You go across the meadow . . ." But it is as yet' an uncultivated " meadow ", yielding nothing but perpetual chief rents to the Industrial Assurance Company which has purchased it from the manorial Mosleys as an investment in real estate, and not very different in appearance from that other clearance area at the opposite end of Great Ancoats Street, which the *Luftwaffe* carried through with less elaborate procedure on a winter night in 1940.   How-ever—air blows over it, yellow coltsfoot marks the coming of Spring, and the willow-herb which follows so swiftly in the wake of destruction, grows as gaily here as in the ruined docks of London River or the open spaces round St.Paul's. And there is certainly more sky in Ancoats than there used to be.

But these undoings and the pursuit of Ancoats neigh-bours to their new estates belong to a later chapter of Settlement history.   We are for the present concerned with Settlement affairs in the years immediately preceding the the second world war, years which were bringing it to the edge of a new crisis and to the end of Mr. and Mrs. Wyatt's gallant and discouraging adventure.

At Christmas 1936 J. L. Stocks resigned from the Vice-Chairmanship and left Manchester to become Vice-Chan-cellor of Liverpool University.   He was succeeded by G. A. Sutherland, Principal of Dalton Hall : a tried friend of the Settlement and a continuing link between it and the Univer-sity.   But J. L. Stocks had loved and tended the Settlement for twelve years.   His life in Manchester was based on the triangle of Wilbraham Road, Ancoats, and the University. His going deprived the Wardens of a philospher and a friend as well as of a very active honorary officer and an expert committee man, and this at a time when finances were once more approaching insolvency. In 1936, £500 more of the Settlement's stock had to be sold to reduce an overdraft. In 1937 the Treasurers viewed with understandable " disappointment and alarm " a deficit of £408. By uncomfortable and discouraging stages the Settlement moved towards a new financial crisis.

It was indeed a complicated crisis. Financial stringency bred anxiety. Anxiety bred doubts as to whether the Settlement was directing its energies aright, with the Corporation pick-axe suspended like a sword of Damocles over its activities. The executive were discouraged ; and at the suggestion of the Vice-Chancellor an outside expert was invited to make an objective report on its work. The resulting document was, however, so objective as to appear to those who lived and worked in Ancoats, wholly irrevelant to its conditions. ' A settlement,' said its author, speaking with the accents of an admonitory schoolmistress, ' must be clean, cheerful, light and colourful.' The Settlement workers had heard that before. The question was, how to make it so on a recurring deficit. The Vice-Chancellor and G.A. Sutherland as its principal officers were faced with a baffling problem of statesmanship and it was fortunate for the Settlement that they were ready to shoulder its burdens. It would have been even more fortunate if J. L. Stocks could have been there to help them ; but his departure to Liverpool had proved to be the first stage of a longer and more irrevocable journey.

After much heartsearching the immediate crisis was met in January, 1940, by the resignation of Mr. Wyatt from his half of the Wardenship, leaving Mrs. Wyatt, with Miss Smellie as sub-Warden, to carry on as best they could with a diminished band of helpers in a world gone mad.

For by this time the Settlement's internal crisis had become part of a greater crisis. Activities had to be switched to wartime needs. The Associates, whose oldest and most faithful members had been grievously depleted by successive deaths, melted away. The Tuesday " at homes " which had survived a first world-war, failed to surmount the rigours of a second. Evening activities became dark and dangerous. Men and women worked themselves tired by day and stayed at home by night. All over Europe—and in Ancoats—the lights went out.

And once more the question was put : can the Settlement survive ?

CHAPTER XI

A NEW CRISIS AND A NEW POLICY

IN January, 1940, the question : " Can the Settlement survive ? " was put to the citizens of Manchester in a pamphlet whose opening paragraph, over the signature of the Vice-Chancellor, and under the heading : *Shall we carry on ?* deserves quotation because of its courage and its brevity.

Although more than half our income has gone, half our neighbours have removed and Ancoats is tumbling down before our eyes, in my view the answer to this question is emphatically yes. Such also was Manchester's answer to this new appeal. And so once more to work.

In spite of the black-out, Ancoats had managed to celebrate Christmas, and under the new wartime title of Citizens Advice Bureau, working in conjunction with the Council of Social Service, the Wardens had been doing what Wardens had always done, war in, war out, in the matter of expert neighbourly advice to individuals. Three valuable basement club-rooms had been taken for an air-raid shelter. Evacuation and slum clearance seemed to have made little difference to the numbers of children to be cared for. They continued to swarm insistently. But from January, 1940, onwards the Settlement was a Warden short. With Miss Smellie as Sub-Warden and Mr. Heath, the experienced organizer of the Pilgrim Club as Club Leader, Mrs. Wyatt held the fort.

Meanwhile, if the Settlement was to carry on, the further question arose : how and where and what was it to carry on ? It was referred to a " Future Policy Sub-Committee " under the Chairmanship of Professor Manson, which provided an answer in May, 1940 :—Since the population of Ancoats was scattering to the new estates, to the new estates must the Settlement follow it. But to which of the new estates ? There were plenty to choose from, and as we have seen, the experiment was not a new one. The Wilbraham Association had grown up under Settlement tutelage and gone its own way. The Newton Heath venture had been abandoned. Its community organization for some reason refused to grow up. For various reasons the Belle Vue Estate at Gorton offered possibilities for the new venture ; among them was the fact that many Ancoats residents were in exile there. And by 'bus along the Hyde Road it was not too inaccessible from the City's centre or from Ancoats. This, however, was to be no mere colony. It was to be a branch of the Settlement ; perhaps in future the heart and centre of it ; at any rate the home of its residents.

To Mrs. Wyatt it fell to make the first tentative moves towards this new adventure. But to others was left the task of carrying it forward ; for in July she and Miss Smellie were appointed to the Staff of the Commandant of the women alien internees' camp in the Isle of Man. For the internees it was a fortunate move. The Summer of 1940 saw the invasion of France and the threatened invasion of Great Britain. The indiscriminate mass internment of aliens which this acute phase of national danger precipitated, resulted in the incarceration of many enlightened and friendly Germans who had taken refuge in this country because they feared and hated Nazi Germany before our own Government thought fit to do so. Their treatment might be justified at the outset as an emergency measure calling for swift action. Their prolonged detention under conditions appropriate for social undesirables and political mischief-makers is perhaps less easy to excuse. But a mitigating factor was the appointment of such people as Mrs. Wyatt to responsible posts in the internment camps. In unofficial conversation with an Aliens' Tribunal member some two years later, one sorely-tried friendly alien was describing with surprising absence of rancour the unhappiness and sense of frustration which she and others like her experienced during this unhappy period. " By the way, did you ever come across Mrs. Wyatt ? " her questioner asked. " Yes indeed," she replied. " I think that was when I first began to feel like a human being again—when I came under Mrs. Wyatt."

Meanwhile a new Warden was installed at the Settlement to develop the new policy : Miss Sheila McKay. She was not new to Ancoats. As one-time Secretary to Miss Cashmore, and as acting Warden during the short interregnum which preceded the coming of Mr. and Mrs. Wyatt, she had learned something of its ways and its climate. During the intervening years she had become familiar with working-class problems as Secretary to Hillcroft Residential College for Working Women. She was young and very energetic. Such qualities were needed, for the Wardenship of the Manchester University Settlement had once again become a pioneering job involving the cultivation of virgin soil and the formation of new social contacts. But in the personnel of its Council, and in its chief honorary officers, there were ˙strong elements of continuity. The Vice-Chancellor as its Chairman and G. A. Sutherland as its Vice-Chairman were still at the helm. Miss A. M. Hewer, one of its oldest residents and a constant steady worker through successive wardenships, was Hon. Treasurer. And of course there was always Mr. Robertson.

Miss McKay entered upon her new kingdom, which was soon to become a dual monarchy and a dispersed one at that, in September, 1940. Before the close of the year there was war in her gates—or at any rate very close to them. In the late autumn the *Luftwaffe* switched its attention from London to the provinces and on the nights of December 22nd and 23rd Manchester received the main force of its attack. Fires ringed the city, bombs rained upon it. The great warehouses of Portland Street and Piccadilly roared up in flame. The thoroughfare which linked Great Ancoats Street to Victoria Bridge became a wilderness. The Royal Exchange was left a smoking shell ; at the meeting place of Market Street and Deansgate the Shambles was a shambles in very deed. The famous dingy old Girls' High School by the University remained intact ; the lovely new building out at Fallowfield, into which it was to move, was left in ruins. There was much to be said for the widening

I

of Piccadilly and the opening of a vista to the Cathedral, but the method of its accomplishment was terrifying and destructive. And that was a fraction of the tale of damage suffered by Manchester during those appalling winter nights. Settlement premises, however, escaped with a bad shaking and a friendly shell-cap through the Round House roof. And Dr. Scholefield's dead were not deceived into thinking that the last trump had sounded; they remained quietly at rest. But even a shaking was enough to seal the fate of the Recreation Room. Its loose timbers became looser; it had at last to go.

Meanwhile shelter life became more abundant in the Round House basement. Scheduled to hold 200 persons, it harboured 300 on particularly menacing dark nights. Meals were served in it. Lectures were held in it. Neighbourly conviviality prevailed in it. The Workers' Educational Association Youth Service campaigned in it. It served, if not the needs of the adjoining streets—since the Housing Committee had disposed of these—at any rate those of many small vulnerable homes within easy reach of it. All of which proved that there was still much work to do in Ancoats, and work the like of which the founders of its Settlement had not foreseen, living as they did in a relatively sane and civilized age.

Thus the year 1940 drew to its fiery close, with, as far as the Settlement was concerned, " faith vindicated " by an " excellent response to the Council's last appeal ", work still to do in Ancoats, and a new field of activity opening out before a new Warden on the Belle Vue Estate at Gorton. To this new field of operations we must now turn our attention.

Where the settlers settle, there is the Settlement; and though activities hummed in the Ancoats premises, the more so since all its rooms were now available for clubs, classes, offices, canteens, bureaux, and shelters, the residents settled at Gorton where, by the continued friendliness of the Corporation Housing Authorities, first one and later two residential flats plus four shops were acquired for Settlement use. In due course eight residents came to be accommodated at 170–4 Stanley Grove. They included the permanent staff of the centre, a floating population of visitors, and student trainees from the Manchester University Social Science Department—and indeed from other social science departments further afield. They did not, however, include the Warden ; that office having become, by now, non-resident. About two years after its first settlement the Gorton Centre secured its community hall, opened on October 31st, 1942, and financed by a joint effort of outside organizations with the tenants themselves contributing a significant quota.

In physical appearance the Belle Vue Estate is much farther from Ancoats than a penny-halfpenny 'bus ride down the Hyde Road would suggest. To Ancoats dwellers it must indeed seem strangely unfamiliar, but with this qualification : lying very close to Belle Vue Garden and the adjoining greyhound-racing track, most people in Manchester have at some time or another sojourned in its near vicinity. With suitable adaptation to larger crowds and smaller purses, Belle Vue Garden provides contemporary Manchester with much the same amenities that Earls Court Exhibition furnished for late Victorian and Edwardian London. And on permitted greyhound racing nights, the neighbouring track has for the last dozen years or so drawn innumerable tram loads, 'bus loads, and motor-car loads of eager punters from all parts of Manchester to what Mr. Winston Churchill once aptly described as " an animated roulette board ". The estate itself lies on the Southern edge of these familiar haunts in an area of wide thoroughfares and surrounding open spaces. Here there are no high overshadowing buildings ; one is conscious of the presence of the sky. But the estate has an accidental unfinished look. Its surrounding open spaces appear rather as urban vacuua than as surviving rural amenities. It has no perceptible middle, no church, no school, no library. These have to be sought on its outskirts. To persons unacquainted with Manchester nomenclature the Settlement's own address may sound misleading, for the word " grove " suggests woodland intimacy, or at any rate a winding shadowy through-route.

There is no sentimental nonsense of this sort about Stanley Grove. Bleak, bare, wide and windy, it cuts ruthlessly through the centre of the estate, its small brick houses with their barren gardens all much of a muchness. It would scarcely be surprising if their inhabitants, some 707 of whom are deportees from Gorton and Ancoats slum clearance areas, preferred the warm convivial huddle of their familiar streets. Happily the majority of them do not. The house is what matters most, and there is no shadow of doubt that these new houses are incomparably better than the old.

For the Settlement worker, however, this particular comparison is less satisfying. There can be no question of falling in love with the Stanley Grove premises at first sight. Here is no romance of history; no tradition to dig up; no whisper of immortal ghostly personalities; no memories either gay or painful. The Settlement workers are as exiled as their neighbours. What do these migrant neighbours want? The worst of it is that at times they do not seem to want anything much—anything that is, that a Settlement can give. And much of what they do want, or ought to want, could be provided—is being provided, not yet adequately but with ever increasing sufficiency— by the statutory social services.

However, the success of the Settlement's pioneer work on the more prosperous, less homogeneous Wilbraham Estate, had been instructive; its apparent failure on the less prosperous, more industrial Newton Heath Estate, had also taught its own lesson. And collective experience on a multitude of similar housing estates up and down Great Britain was piling up. It was the business of those responsible for the Gorton Centre not merely to accumulate such experience and use it, but to add to it. And for a beginning, it was decided to push ahead with the task which the Settlement Survey Committee had broken off on the eve of the war after completing the first part of its great slum clearance enquiry: the part which recorded and analysed the circumstances of families leaving Ancoats. Part two remained: the follow-up which should throw light on their subsequent fortunes.

It was not practicable under wartime conditions to complete the whole projected programme of following up the individual Ancoats families in all their various directions. But with an active group of workers established on the Belle Vue Estate it was at any rate thought possible to make an intensive survey of this one small area and achieve thereby some standard of comparison with earlier conditions.   And this would have the added advantage of bringing the Settlement workers into closer touch with their new neighbourhood, its ways, its thoughts, and its needs.   Accordingly in 1942 a new Survey Committee set to work under Miss Remington, then Sub-Warden in charge of the Gorton Centre, and with some previous experience of survey work.

The result of their efforts was a detailed and highly informative pamphlet,[1] describing the outlay and general social composition of the Belle Vue Estate and including in its scope a large block of Corporation flats in the near neighbourhood.   Perhaps its most useful feature, at any rate for social workers on the Estate, is its careful record of the tenants' own views concerning their new surroundings :   their likes and dislikes ;   their conscious needs ; their dominating preoccupations.

With such knowledge as a starting-point a young generation of workers :   systematic students and practitioners of social science, is setting out upon this newest major venture of the Manchester University Settlement.   Clubs and drama, adult education and expert neighbourly advice, all the old familiar activities have come swiftly into production. Only the times and the places are strange.   But since we have reached the point where the history impinges on the current and as yet unsolved problems of the Belle Vue Centre, we must here take leave of it.   Let us do so with the reminder that pioneers in a new world do not always find what they seek or do what they intend.   Their discoveries are often surprising, their achievements unexpected ;   and the latter

[1] *A Survey of Housing and Social Amenities on Belle Vue, Gorton, New Housing Estate, 1942-3.* Published by the Manchester University Settlement, price 6d.

are likely to be conditioned by a compromise with the unpredictable exigencies of climate.

If the brief story of the Gorton Centre has to be concluded with a question mark, so too does the long story of what has now become the Ancoats Centre. Of what is it the centre ? Of a small territory suggesting by its barrenness the track of an invading army : a territory surrounded in its turn by the entanglement of mills, warehouses, and mean streets left over by the Industrial Revolution, with the impedimenta of the great Railway Age superimposed upon it. Some day this encircling mess will be tidied up and sorted out. The remaining mean streets will go the way of Every Street ; homes and workshops will be disentangled. The process would of course be easier in Moscow than in Manchester where the complications of inflated site-values and inelastic chief rents cramp the style of planners round the City's centre. And it would doubtless have been swifter had there been no war to create irresistible priority demands on the nation's building resources. But it is at any rate the declared intention of the Corporation to rehouse at least some of the Settlement's evicted neighbours in 380 flats erected on their native soil. Some day these things will happen.

Meanwhile there are streets enough within reach to keep the Ancoats Centre full and busy. And maybe, as time goes on, like Toynbee Hall in London it will draw increasing strength from still wider areas. More and more will it serve, indeed it has always served, as a home of study and debate, of social service enterprise, and art and drama. Maybe the " scorched earth " encircling the Round House will some day be a verdant open space, of which it will be no mockery to say to the enquirer : " You go across the meadow . . ."

But the Gorton Centre started its life, and the Ancoats Centre renewed its life under the shadow of war ; with the abnormalities of war conditioning the activities of both. By the time this record sees the light, that shadow may have lifted to disclose a busy scene of social reconstruction and liberated man-power—or not, as the case may be. For the present, to the ancient question " Watchman, what of the night ? " there comes only the enigmatic answer recorded by the Prophet : " The morning cometh, and also the night : if ye will enquire, enquire ye."

CHAPTER XII

THE WAR YEARS

THE war years, which coincided with the third great era of constructive effort in the history of the M.U.S., impelled many of its responsible officers to set themselves the task of defining the functions of a University Settlement in the world of to-day. The Warden herself engages in such an attempt in the opening paragraph of her report for 1942-3.

" A University Settlement has," she says, " traditionally six main functions. It provides a centre for neighbourhood social life and the opportunity for learning the duties and responsibilities of citizenship in a democratic community ; it provides a common and informal meeting ground for people of different educational and social backgrounds ; it gives advice and help to anxious and troubled people who are bewildered by official regulations and domestic upheavals, especially in wartime ; it acts as a liaison between the man-in-the-street and the officials of statutory and other organizations which affect his life ; it carries out educational and social experiments and undertakes research into social conditions ; it takes responsibility for training students in practical social work."

The list of activities appended to this definition of purpose makes it clear that in the year 1943 the M.U.S. was actively engaged in the discharge of all these functions.

With one exception they might stand as the programme of work which stretched into the future before the eyes of the first settlers at the close of last century. They are, as she says, traditional. There are, of course, changes of emphasis which reflect the march of intervening events and have brought about the changes of atmosphere and personnel described at the outset of this narrative. Of this, perhaps the outstanding example is the way in which the present leaders of the M.U.S. interpret the function of providing a centre for neighbourhood social life and an informal meeting place for persons of different educational background. Its Development Committee [1] is of opinion that " the perpetuation of the idea of a community house is undesirable. Settlement workers should live in simple houses or flats like those ordinarily resident in the neighbourhood " ; and students " might be billeted with the local residents ". This repudiation of a permanently established community inspired by a resident Warden in a house capable of setting new standards of spaciousness and grace, would have surprised the pioneers. But the thought of billets among the neighbours would probably have surprised them still more and possibly intimidated them somewhat. True, their neighbours were worse housed and maybe wilder. And of course to-day we are dealing with a generation of students to whom such billeting is a familiar wartime experience. Many of them have already achieved at the bench or in the barrack-room, effortless and easy contacts with working-class interests—or lack of them. For them there is no need to " make contact " or to affect such elaborate disguises as Mrs. Sidney Webb was forced to adopt in order to gain first-hand experience of working-class life. The aim, of the modern Settlement may, in this respect, be " traditional ". Its method is not.

There is, however, little or no break with tradition in the desire to inculcate the " duties and responsibilities of citizenship in a democratic community ". There are doubtless more of them, owing to the enormously expanded range of state action ; and more people have them, thanks to the extension of the franchise. Moreover, recent history has provided two spectacular examples of what may happen to a nation whose people repudiate such responsibilities. So this particular job goes forward : as urgent as ever it was and perhaps no nearer to completion.

This same expansion in the range of state action has also increased both the magnitude and the urgency of the Settlement's third traditional function : that of giving " advice

[1] See their *Interim Memorandum* dated 7th June, 1944.

and help to anxious and troubled people who are bewildered by official regulations and domestic upheavals " and of acting as a " liaison between the man-in-the-street and the officials of statutory organizations ". In the days when the elementary school teacher, the relieving officer and the sanitary inspector represented the state's concern for the individual's standard of life, settlement workers were perhaps less conscious of the need for contact with the statutory authorities than of the hungry, barefoot, workhouse-shadowed primary poverty which resulted from their impotence. But for one reason or another there were always " anxious and troubled people ".

As to the fifth traditional function : educational and social experiment and research—there it always was and here it is. Social legislation and administration still have far to go before the material conditions of a good life are within reach of all ; and as we have seen, the unrelaxing experiments and researches of two generations of settlement workers have helped to build up such social legislation as we have. But to-day their researches involve more external contacts and command more systematic guidance than was formerly the case, and their experiments are better publicised.

So far, then, the functions of a University Settlement remain much as they were conceived half a century ago. But the pioneers would have noticed a hiatus in the modern redefinition, and the moderns have added a sixth function which the pioneers knew not.

First and foremost among the objects of the Manchester Art Museum and University Settlement as redefined in 1901 stands the resolve " to disseminate and nourish a healthy love of Nature and of the best in Art, Music, Literature and Science among the industrial population of Manchester. . . ." This aim is present only by implication in our contemporary statement of functions. It may be replied that the Settlement was at this earlier date a composite institution, and that this cultural priority aim represents the contribution of the Horsfall Art Museum to its dual personality. There is, however, more to it than that. It was, as we have seen, the aim which took precedence in the minds and

activities of the early Settlement workers. They lived and
worked under the shadow of Ruskin, Morris, De Morgan,
and Walter Crane. An early Warden, Guy Kendall, throws
some light on the matter in his recently published memoirs.[1]
He quotes the statement of a women's college principal
that when girls talked of " realizing themselves " they meant
" going to Italy ", and adds :—" Certainly in those days
we regarded ' going to Italy ' as a very necessary part of
culture." Octavia Hill went to Italy. Alice Crompton
went to Italy. And the service of one's fellow human
beings was best conceived as handing on the æsthetic and
intellectual culture that one had absorbed there. Ruskin
was the great bridge-builder between culture and philanthropy, and Ruskin was full of Italy. It was not only
through the medium of Horsfall and his Art Museum that
Ruskin shed his light in Ancoats but through Octavia
Hill, the Barnetts and the Settlement movement as a
whole.

To the Settlement worker of the inter-war period " self-
realization " was more likely to be connected with a visit
to Soviet Russia or the working-class tenements of Vienna.
We had by then moved forward into the age of social science
and its widespread systematic study, an age of increasing
preoccupation with the analysis of cause as a necessary
preliminary to any individual attack upon effect. And in
such an age, to sow the seeds of æsthetic culture in ground
ill-prepared for their reception may seem to involve waste
of effort. It is of course presumptuous and perhaps irre-
ligious to say that any human effort of service is wasted,
since who knows what world-wide repercussions may be
transmitted through individual response to it, or what may
be its valuation in the realm of the spirit. But it is certainly
true that the æsthetic activities of the pioneers left little
impress on the poverty-ridden homes of Ancoats, whereas
the demonstrations of interior house-decoration with which
the Corporation Housing Committee crowned its large-
scale rehousing programme, have resulted in a luxuriant
outcrop of Van Gogh reproductions and a revolt against

[1] *A Headmaster Remembers*, by Guy Kendall.

Nottingham lace curtains throughout the newly-built suburbs of Manchester.

At any rate, the substitution of Miss McKay's sixth function for the pioneer's first, is significant of the most considerable change of emphasis which half a century has wrought in Settlement life. It has brought a new breed of student trainee settlers into the picture : fleeting settlers, settlers with ulterior motives, settlers whose present pre-occupations and projected activities link their Settlements ever more closely, entangle their activities and their finances ever more inextricably, with the statutory social services and large grant-aided voluntary bodies for whose development the Settlements themselves are so largely responsible.

And now, having discussed the functions of a Settlement and of Settlements in general, let us face the possibility that such definitions are irrelevant or at any rate of limited value. Our doubts are stirred by an address [1] to fellow-workers given by J. L. Stocks on the eve of his departure from Manchester. What are Settlements for ? He is inclined to think that the question should not be put like this at all " since the best things are not for anything in particular ". For instance : " It is easy enough to say what a saw is for : it has a simple perfectly definite function and it is good according as it performs this function. . . . Even a human being if he is a slave can be regarded similarly : his purposes are those of his master. But a free man resents it if we ask him what he is for. To him, at least, though to others this may seem an exaggeration, his existence is its own justifica-tion : he is, as the philosopher said, an end in himself. Perhaps a similar distinction should be made among insti-tutions. Many have a perfectly definite aim, e.g. to abolish slavery, to establish free trade, to relieve destitution, and they succeed as they fulfil these objects. But others, and these are the most essential, lack any such definite aim, though they may incidentally contribute to each and all. The human family is such an institution, existing for no

[1] *Why do we believe in Settlements ?* Printed in the M.U.S. Annual Report, 1935–6.

single purpose, but creating a common life for its members
and thus standing on a basis as broad as life itself ; enjoying
success so far as the quality of the life which it creates
and maintains is good. What I suggest is that a Settlement is an institution of this type, and that the lack of a
definable aim or purpose is a sign of strength and not of
weakness."

This " quality of life " is, however, difficult to measure,
and when events and achievements have been duly recorded,
and functions duly taped, it remains elusive. John Masefield, in his poem *Biography*, reminds us that the external
record of his life " reduced to dates and facts " will tell us
little of its really significant moments.

> " And none will know the gleam there used to be
> About the feast days freshly kept by me,
> But men will call the hour of golden bliss
>   ' About this time ' or ' shortly after this '.

So, too, in the biography of the M.U.S. whose " quality
of life " is its own justification, the most significant " hours
of golden bliss " may go unrecorded, and what Masefield
calls " the sprinkled seeds " may germinate unmarked. We
can seek for them in the memories of individuals who have
touched that institution at some point in their lives, but
even so we cannot measure their potency or analyse their
effects. Our search ends in a jumble of fragmentary experience. Voices reach us in many accents, sometimes
from great distances :—" It was *there* that I first saw what
unemployment really meant . . ."—" It was *there* I was
first moved to go and train . . ."—" It was *there* I found that
I could act . . ."—" It was *there* I learned to read poetry
. . ."—" It was *there* I met C. P. Scott . . . Samuel
Alexander . . . Margaret Ashton . . . Jimmy Mallon . . ."
—" It was *there* that Aylmer Maude used to talk to us of
Tolstoy . . ."—" It was *there* that I saw Ellen Terry when
she came to our Tuesday ' at home ' in a yellow linen dress
and a huge great amber necklace . . ."—" It was *there* I

met my wife . . ."—" *There* I found my friend . . ."—
" It was *there* that he and I worked together, and every brick
of its building, every turn of the streets that lead to it
recalls his personality and the times we had there. . . ."

CHAPTER XIII

AFTER THE WAR

NINETEEN-FORTY-FIVE was the year of the Settlement's golden jubilee; it was also the year that saw the end of the Second World War and the drafting of much of our post-war social legislation. The roots of the welfare state lie, of course, much deeper, but the new legislation introduced many features that were to change the pattern of our system of public welfare, and were in particular to have a profound influence on the life and activity of most voluntary organizations.

In the first place, a co-ordinated legislative system came into being by which the state bore the responsibility for supporting the individual through most of the major vicissitudes of life. The national insurance system, supported by family allowances and the National Assistance Board, provided a " national minimum "; the health service was responsible for making sure that none should be deprived of the best service that modern medicine could provide; in the field of formal education the educational system was committed to " equality of opportunity ", and in the development of community centres and youth work Education authorities were to enter into the recreational life of the community. Beside this basic programme there was a considerable extension of services for the handicapped and for children bereft of normal care. And, of course, a huge housing programme was, in the main, already planned. It was clear therefore that voluntary organizations of all kinds, and settlements in particular, would not, in the future, be called upon to do many of the things that they had done in the past.

The second factor was more subtle. The new welfare legislation had, on the one hand, taken from the local authorities much of the responsibility they had borne in the past. They were no longer responsible for institutional medical care, or for the relief of distress ; but, on the other hand, they were given very considerable powers in other ways. Under many of the post-war Acts local authorities were made responsible for ensuring that the welfare services in their areas were adequate ; indeed, they could, if they wished, undertake almost any kind of welfare work themselves. In fact, the future was to see clubs for old people, information centres, youth centres, clubs for the handicapped all run by local authorities, on whose payrolls were to be found : youth leaders, community centre wardens and special case workers for old people and for problem families. In other words, there were now comparatively few fields of social work which voluntary organizations could claim as their sole preserve. One effect of this was to introduce a healthy competitive element into the field of social work, and particularly was this so when local medical officers of health, shorn of their administrative responsibilities for hospital organization, were led to concentrate more of their energies on the enormous field of social medicine. Voluntary organizations could, of course, act as agents for the local authorities in the undertaking of many of these duties, and the vast majority of local authorities wholeheartedly welcomed the presence within their boundaries of a reservoir of experience and expertise which could be drawn upon immediately for these tasks and to give grants to those societies that could do the jobs. They were, moreover, encouraged to do so by Whitehall. Many, too, with commendable modesty, felt that certain tasks could be more effectively undertaken by voluntary agencies than by public bodies, and were content to occupy the role of patron rather than that of promoter.

The post-war welfare state was, in 1945, a welfare state only on paper. It was clear that growing pains would affect the final plan, and most voluntary organizations were content to wait to see what would happen. But this was not always possible, and it was certainly not possible for the Settlement to do so, for some very important decisions on future policy had to be made in advance of the stabilization of national post-war development.

The Settlement, in the immediate pre-war years, had in some measure been dominated by the policy of dispersal. It had felt that it might well serve a greater need in the new housing estates than in the old centre in Ancoats. During the war years it had, moreover, ceased to be a residential settlement in the full, accepted sense of the term, for its residence was small and was not, in fact, the place where the warden lived. The reasons for the pre-war and wartime decisions were, in the light of pre-war social policy, good, for under pre-war slum clearance policy Ancoats as a residential centre had largely disappeared. But post-war plans were to repeople Ancoats, and from one end of Every Street to the other, and in the hinterland on either side, three-storied blocks of flats were to be erected by the Housing Department of the City Corporation, as part of their housing plan. The people who were to occupy them, however, would not necessarily be Ancoats folk ; they would be those who were high on the official housing list, and it would be some time before they would become a real community. On the great housing estates with which the city was to be surrounded, the forging of that social bond which binds people from many different parts into a self-conscious group with local pride was to be stimulated by the new community association community centres, but in Ancoats it must clearly be the work of the Settlement. Moreover, the Settlement's property was, in the main, in Ancoats, right in the centre of the new developments.

Thus with 1945 there came a problem, and it was a problem that could not wait for a solution until the pattern of post-war social policy would become clear. Furthermore, settlements, more than most voluntary organizations, are dependent for the direction of their activities and the formulation of policy almost entirely upon the personality, ability and interests of their wardens. It is the warden who leads the " settlers " and it is he who has his finger on the pulse of local life, and is thus in touch with local needs. He, moreover, sees social legislation in action and is better able than most folk in the area to assess its success or failure. His sensitivity to local needs makes him a local

K

leader and, in large measure, he will be the focus of local aspiration. The warden was, therefore, a key to future policy. But Miss McKay, who had striven so valiantly with the social problems of the war, was to leave, in order, with her great experience and gentle understanding, to stimulate the growing movement for the establishment of community centres.

The last major task that Miss McKay undertook was the organization of the celebrations that were to mark the Settlement's year of Jubilee. Of necessity this had to be a big affair and Manchester responded nobly. The *Manchester Guardian* published an article on the Settlement and other journals, like *Social Welfare*, the organ of the Manchester and Salford Council of Social Service, opened their pages to contributions about it. The great occasions, however, were the University Council's reception in the Whitworth Hall, when J. J. Mallon, the pioneer settler that Ancoats had given to Toynbee Hall, gave a reminiscent and exciting address, and the performance, on two occasions, of Mrs. Stocks's play—*Dr. Scholefield*—with Jeffrey Dean, a loyal and reliable (albeit retiring) friend of the Settlement, in the title role.

These were highly successful ventures, but it would have been a lifeless voluntary society that let a jubilee go by without asking for money, and the Settlement set out, with vigour and enthusiasm, to create a Jubilee Fund. This was successful and a total figure of £1,080 was achieved.

The new Warden, R. E. Reedman, came to Ancoats on April 10th, 1945, and it would be right to think of that date as marking the beginning of the Settlement's post-war history. Ralph Reedman was a man of experience and imagination and he was supported by a wife who was to be much loved in Ancoats for her thoughtfulness for others and for the gentle dignity that she brought into everyday life. During the war he had been in the Navy, but earlier he had been a very successful warden of the Educational Settlement at Maryport in Cumberland, a settlement which had come into being in the dark days of unemployment in between the wars. Ancoats was, of course, a different proposition

and Reedman had to find his way through the complexities
of a somewhat indefinite situation. He had, too, to come
to grips with the dilemma that has already been mentioned.
By this time, the liveliness of activity in Every Street had
made it abundantly clear that in the claims on the Settlement Ancoats was not going to play second fiddle to Gorton.
The simple solution would have been to expand the Settlement's activities in both places, but rising costs and a mount-
ing deficit could not really admit of this policy. The
Warden and the Council had to decide what they were
going to do and where they were going to do it.

On October 23rd, 1947, a committee was set up to in-
vestigate the matter. It was a powerful committee and was
driven hard under the chairmanship of a second Lawrence
Scott, who had recently become treasurer. He had been a
" settler " himself and had lived at Toynbee Hall, so he
brought to the investigation not only the energy of an active
proprietor of the *Manchester Guardian*, but also the sympathy and sensitivity of one who knew what settlements
were for. The committee worked extremely hard, holding
eleven meetings between October 1947 and March 1948.
Its report was remarkable and was to have far-reaching
results. It argued that :—

A settlement should serve the neighbourhood in which
it is situated.

A settlement should provide a meeting place for people
from different classes.

A settlement should provide a field for pioneering social
work.

and using these principles as a touchstone, it assessed the
work that the Settlement was doing and laid down a policy
for the future. The argument in favour of this " new
look " was in some measure a financial one. The Settlement had been losing money and the committee were
anxious that its activities should be confined within its
means. But the argument did not rest there ; the committee
were also concerned that the work which the Settlement
was doing should be well done and that adequate finance

should be available for it.   To meet these two points it was better to concentrate the Settlement's financial resources and to reduce the scale of the programme.   The spread of activity was reaching the point where it was dangerously near being both uneconomic and inefficient. It argued, further, that as the Settlement was now clearly needed in Ancoats, its old home, then Ancoats must be its first responsibility and that it would be better to sacrifice the work at Gorton in the interest of concentration and extension of the activities in Every Street.   The size of the staff that could be employed was also a limiting factor, for the committee came with reluctance to the conclusion that a Warden, a Secretary, and one other was the maximum that the Settlement could afford if it was going to employ, and pay for, good workers.   If more workers were to be employed, their salaries must be guaranteed in full from other sources.

One of the most interesting suggestions, however, was that the " residence " should be re-established in Ancoats in a different form.   Residents would, in future, be housed in three places instead of one.   Some would live in Ancoats Hall, some in the Round House, and some in a flat in one of the new blocks that were being built by the Corporation in Every Street.   This was a far-sighted suggestion.   Some settlements had discovered that a large residence can become a community in itself, with its own life and activity, and in so doing lose touch with the neighbourhood.   The new plan of " offence in breadth " would obviate this, for though the residents would come together at meal times and for work in the Round House, they would at other times be citizens of Ancoats on the same basis as their neighbours.

The reduction in the size of the staff would, of course, also mean that some of the Settlement's work would also have to go.   Accordingly, and with much heart-searching, it was decided that work among young people between the ages of fourteen and eighteen could be left to other youth organizations in the district, and that the Settlement should concentrate its activities on children and adults.   It was visualized that a first-class children's play centre should be created and that a determined effort should be made to meet the needs of older people. Such a recommendation was bound to be a difficult one for a settlement to accept, for settlements claim, above everything else, to cater for the needs of the whole family, and any settlement would find it very difficult to contemplate cutting out such an important age group. As it turned out, this recommendation was never implemented, but in rejecting it the Council was making a great act of faith, for the years to come were to show clearly that the salary of the extra worker involved was a burden which was to continue the annual, deficit. The " Scott " report, as it came to be called, had, in fact, pinpointed the most shaky point in the organization's position.

The reconstitution of the work in Ancoats and the re-establishment of the residence meant a considerable amount of work for Ralph Reedman. The Round House, which had been a British Restaurant during the war, had to be redecorated, and in some measure reconstructed ; the residence at Ancoats Hall had to be reorganized, and furniture had to be collected for both places. But the settlement activities were flourishing, and he had to be a settlement warden as well. He did both jobs with energy and insight and this in spite of the fact that he had decided that he could not commit himself to work in Ancoats for the period of five years which he felt was necessary to bring the plans to full fruition. He had come to this decision slowly and with great responsibility and he balanced carefully the Settlement's needs with his own. He promised to supervise the alterations and to stay till his successor had been appointed, and so to make his successor's path as smooth as the path of the warden of a settlement ever can be. He left on March 31st, 1949, almost exactly four years after he had come to Ancoats, and all who knew him felt that the County Education Committee of Kent were extremely fortunate to get so good a man. He was thoughtful, and, in a way, self-effacing ; he possessed a deep understanding of education, and he could think clearly in terms of policy. He was sensitive to the needs of others, as his care for the needs of his successor showed.

The way in which a settlement's activities are affected by the personality of the warden was clearly seen in Reedman's successor—Gordon Kidd, the present Warden—a man of a very different temperament and outlook. True, he, too, came from an educational settlement that had sprung up to serve the needs of an area scarred by the blight of unemployment, in the Welsh mountain town of Bryn Mawr. But he had been much more closely associated with youth clubs than his predecessor had been, and though his horizon was not by any means limited by this, he was naturally enough more reluctant to accept this particular recommendation of the Scott Report. Indeed, he saw this as the one weakness of the report, and he persuaded the Executive Committee and the Council to agree with him. So it came about that after long deliberation the post of Youth Leader was again written into the list of Settlement staff. Though none now regrets this decision, it is nevertheless true that the subsequent financial difficulties of the Settlement have been bound up with it.

Gordon Kidd's most unusual quality is an empirical one. He is able quickly to grasp the possibilities of a situation, to see needs as they arise, and to feel his way to a solution. The arguments to support his decisions will come later, but they will be found good. The summer camp is a good example of this. Kidd introduced this largely as a part of the youth clubs' programme, but he was quick to see its possibilities for the Settlement as a whole and in the years to come it was to become one of the focal points of the Settlement's life.

It was round Gordon Kidd's enthusiastic personality that the new settlement and the new residence were to be built, and it was built upon good foundations. As a good warden, he had of course to do his own building, but he would, I am sure, be the first to pay tribute to the work that had been done before he came. One of the things he inherited was a remarkably good group of residents who had been living at Gorton. This group were not only keen settlement workers, but they were also active in the student life of the University, and they were soon joined by a group who were similarly active in the College of Technology. Thus a closer link was forged between the student life of Manchester and the Settlement, a link that still exists and which is, probably, stronger than in any other settlement in the country.

The residence was in some measure redesigned according to suggestions made by the new warden who was now to live in a flat in the Round House itself. The bulk of the residents lived in Ancoats Hall but a small and active group lived in " The Flat ". This flat was to become something of a small settlement on its own, and it is very heartening to see how the children of the area seem to think that it belongs to them, and not to the residents.

With the exception of the development of youth work, the settlement's work proceeded, more or less, according to plan. Under the leadership of Miss Joyce Haworth—a lecturer on the staff of the University Faculty of Education as well as a Settlement worker—the Play Centre became a model one, catering for large numbers of very young children almost every day of the week. But Miss Haworth did more. Before she came the chief day-to-day link between the Settlement and the University had been the close contact which had always been maintained between the Settlement and the Social Administration Department of the University, whose students and staff were always in touch with what was happening in Every Street, and were usually involved in many of the Settlement's activities. This is a natural relationship, and one which still persists, but Miss Haworth, together with the indefatigable secretary of the Settlement, Miss Coulthard, brought the whole Faculty of Education into the picture as supporters of the Settlement, and so tied even closer the bonds that make the M.U.S. a real university settlement. The work among adults was mainly the responsibility of the Warden, but in this he was assisted by another member of the staff, who had not been officially appointed, and who was certainly not paid : his wife, who led clubs, visited old people, undertook casework, and acted as a housekeeper whenever needed. Her work was later recognized (when she was officially appointed as Girls' Club Leader) but the desire so to recognize it was not hers, it was that of the Executive Committee, which slowly became more shamefaced at the thought of leaning so heavily on such gracious and efficient, but unacknowledged, support.

The Settlement did all the things that a good neighbourhood centre should do. It became the centre of all the important social activities in Ancoats ; it was a Citizens' Advice Bureau ; it ran the Red Cross Loan Depot ; the Probation Officers used it as a Report Centre, and it became the home of local societies and adult classes. It provided, moreover, an understanding home for people who wanted to talk about Ancoats, and who would always find in Gordon Kidd a sympathetic listener. But it did many other things as well. The most remarkable of these was its entry into a different field of service altogether ; it bought a second-hand motor-coach.

This was a really outstanding venture. At first few but the Warden, who undertook to drive the bus, saw its potentialities, and the purchase, though provided for by special contributions from such bodies as the University Unions, was again an act of faith in the Warden by the Council. It was to have a remarkable effect on the Settlement's work for it made the settlement idea mobile. The children from the Play Centre could now be brought into real contact with the countryside, and they could even become familiar with the parks which the city provides but which are so scarce in Ancoats ; the Settlement camp could not only be organized more easily, but it now became available for all members of Settlement Clubs, and for the very first time in this country members of old people's clubs were taken away for an annual holiday, under canvas. And this old bus also became a formidable instrument in the cause of education, for it took parties of people, both young and old, from the dark chasms of Ancoats streets into the sun-drenched pastures of the upper Alps, and many Parisians must have glanced with surprise at the sight of a blue and white coach bearing the coat of arms of a noble university and the words " Manchester University Settlement " driving triumphantly down the Avenue de l'Opéra.

The bus was used as a cheap form of transport only when

it was felt that the work of the Settlement would be enhanced by it. It catered for needs that would not otherwise be met ; it increased the scope of the Settlement's activities during the summer months, and as an instrument of foreign travel it was extending that field of informal education which settlements have always felt to be their particular care. Incomes in Ancoats had increased, and families who had, in the past, known only " the holiday " of worklessness and penury were able to leave their mills and factories behind and for a week or a fortnight be away from work and free from worry at the same time. This was an educational opportunity, and the glimpse of life in foreign lands widened the horizon of many, but this would never have been achieved without the intervention of the Settlement, and its bus. These trips, moreover, stimulated the demand for more formal activity, and classes in foreign languages and geography have now found their way into the Settlement's curriculum.

In a way, too, the bus enabled the Settlement to do more efficiently something which it had always set itself out to do. In 1915 it had started a holiday school for children. In 1920 the children of Ancoats were taken to Didsbury gardens by tram, and later in the 20's settlement parties visited Paris and Geneva. It had always been felt that it was a good thing to take people away from Ancoats. The M.U.S. of the 1950's is better equipped to do this than ever before.

The post-war years have not, of course, been lacking in difficulty. Finance was always a problem, but in these years it has been particularly acute. To some extent the Executive Committee and 'the Council must accept responsibility for this, for if they had been more determined in their attempts to limit the Settlement's work, it might have been possible to avoid deficits. But they were also clear-sighted enough to see that an organization that is developing, that is showing imagination, and that is clearly growing in prestige should not be confined in this way. So they have been faced with the alternative of killing a living and vital thing, or of being courageous in their approach to finance, even to the point of danger. In one sense this is the wisest course, for the income of a dying organization will in time also die, but the income of a vital one will increase ; and in spite of the fact that there has been a deficit in each of the post-war years, and sometimes this has been a heavy one, the income has also grown, and grown considerably.

This type of financial problem is, of course, a recurrent one as far as voluntary organizations are concerned, and with energy and faith it can usually be met. But within the last two years of the decade the position has been aggravated by what is, for the Settlement, a tragic, historical accident : Ancoats Hall acquired a new landlord.

Since the Settlement entered on its " Golden Age ", Ancoats Hall had been its home, and though for most of this time the greater part of the building was used by the Art Gallery Committee of the City Council, and the Settlement occupied only one wing, that wing was nevertheless an essential part of the organization's life and activity. The City Fathers had, moreover, been kind to the Settlement, for with a contribution to the city's rates they were content, they did not ask a rent. In 1953, however, they decided that the Horsfall museum would serve the city better if it were housed in the city centre. Accordingly, they surrendered the lease to the ground landlord—British Railways —" a king who knew not Joseph ". He made plans to use the building himself, as a model recreational centre for railwaymen from the Manchester Depots, but he was happy that the Settlement residence should continue to occupy its corner, at a " commercial rent ". The sting was in the tail, for a commercial rent of over £140 a year was a crippling blow for an organization already working to an annual deficit. And the blow was even heavier than this, in that the rent was coupled to a clause making the Settlement responsible for structural repairs, and the graceful old building at the corner of Every Street could be a heavy liability.*

This problem has still to be solved, but in the sixty

---

* Since this account went to press, British Railways, as ground landlords, have reconsidered the whole position, and have proposed another agreement which is both understanding and very generous.

years of its life the M.U.S. has never been cowed by problems.

The last ten years has of course also seen many changes in the faces that help to run the Settlement. Sir John Stopford, as chairman of the Council, has continued to give himself unsparingly to the Settlement, but some grand old supporters have passed on. Among these, the two names which arouse most memories are those of H. Pilkington Turner and G. St. Claire Robertson, two pioneers who built better than they knew. But as old supporters passed, new ones took their place. In 1945 George Sutherland, whose memorable "temporary" chairmanship of seven years must be a record, handed over the reins of the Executive Committee to Edna Lind, the warden of Ashburne Hall, who brought to the Settlement administration the keenness of a scientist's brain and a sensitivity acquired from many years of voluntary social work. It was she who guided the Settlement through most of these difficult years, until in December 1951 she left to undertake pioneer work in one of the new universities in Africa. After a short inter-regnum she was succeeded by the present chairman, Professor W. Mansfield Cooper, a man whom Ancoats could almost claim as its own, for he was educated at an elementary school nearby, and through the W.E.A. and Ruskin College has climbed to one of the most illustrious positions in the land, for he is to be the University's next Vice Chancellor.

Under the leadership of such a keen Warden as Gordon Kidd the work that the Settlement is still going to do will be well done. Settlements represent the consumers of social services. Their workers are part of the neighbourhood, they know what is good and what is not so good in the operation of the "welfare state" and in using that knowlege to improve it can claim their rightful place within it.

APPENDIX

UNIVERSITY SETTLEMENT WARDENS

From the panel placed in the Round House

1896. ERNEST CAMPAGNAC and C. HELÈNE STOEHR.
1898. ALICE CROMPTON and SIDNEY MCDOUGALL.
1900. ALICE CROMPTON and GUY KENDALL.
1901. ALICE CROMPTON and T. R. MARR.
1909. J. H. WHITEHOUSE.
1912. GRAHAM V. COX.
1913. G. K. GRIERSON.
1917. BEATRICE B. ROGERS.
1926. HILDA CASHMORE.
1931. HILDA CASHMORE and LADY MABEL SMITH.
1933. RENDEL H. WYATT and JEAN C. WYATT.
1940. SHEILA S. MCKAY.
1945. R. E. REEDMAN.
1949. GORDON KIDD.

INDEX

138

INDEX TO THE SECOND EDITION

*Items and Names which already appear in the index.